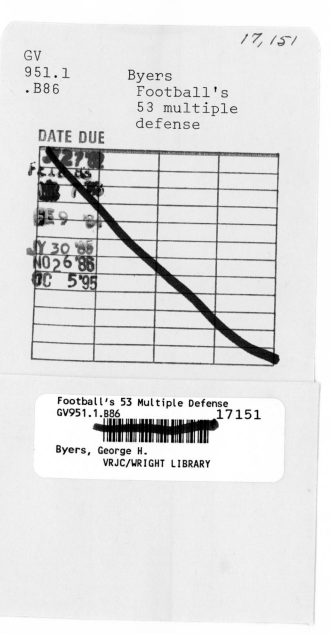

Football's 53
Multiple Defense

© 1973, *by*

PARKER PUBLISHING COMPANY, INC.

West Nyack, N.Y.

Library of Congress Cataloging in Publication Data

Byers, George H
  Football's 53 multiple defense.

  1. Football--Defense. I. Title.
GV951.1.B86   796.33'22   72-12536
ISBN 0-13-324707-4

Printed in the United States of America

Football's 53 Multiple Defense

George H. Byers

Parker Publishing Company, Inc.
West Nyack, N.Y.

DEDICATION

. To my father Herman Byers for teaching me the basic fundamentals and coverages of the original 53 Corner Defense which is the core of the 53 Multiple Defense.

. To Bill Gonzales for doing an outstanding job as defensive line coach, and to our Irvington "Hell Raisers" (defensive unit) for their outstanding play and dedication.

. To my wife Joyce for her patience, understanding, and support as the wife of a dedicated high school football coach.

How This Book Will Help
You Win More Games

Multiple defensive football, in my opinion, is a necessity in defensing modern offensive football teams. Today's offensive teams pose more problems for the defense. Through multiple offensive formations and men in motion, and new offensive innovations such as the belly option, offensive teams continue to harass and confuse the defense.

To counter this problem, defensive coaches must innovate new defensive ideas to demoralize modern offensive teams. I believe that the 53 Multiple Defense with its tremendous flexibility is an answer towards solving many of the problems confronting today's modern defensive coach.

It is very difficult, unless the defense has superior personnel, to stay in the same basic defense for an entire game and get the job done. A well-drilled offensive team that can anticipate both the same defensive alignment and defensive techniques from down to down will pick this defense apart.

When we first began with our 53 defense, we ran one basic defense. Initially, we had great success with our basic 53, leading our league in both team defense and pass defense. However, as we progressed with the 53 we found that we had to add variations to make it more flexible, for two reasons. First, we had to be more flexible in meeting new offensive trends, and second, we had to adapt our style of defensive play to fit in with the physical capabilities of the personnel available.

As we developed our 53 Multiple Defense it became both a multiple and a moving defense—multiple in the sense that we alter the defensive alignment as we adjust to various offensive game conditions, and moving in that we change our defensive alignment both before and during the snap of the ball.

Moving defensive football has been very good for us. Like many high school and college football teams, we had to use small men versus opponents with physically larger and stronger men. By moving on the snap of the ball, our small but quick men have been able to confuse offensive blockers and stymie the modern day offense. Thus, we do a lot of attacking and stunting within our defensive system of play. As a result of our moving defense, we have been able to compensate quite well versus teams that have out-manned us. For this reason we are sold on moving defensive football. This book will illustrate to the defensive coach how he can use a small but quick man who is aggressive, to great advantage through moving defensive football.

A sound defensive team must have the flexibility to adjust during actual game conditions. This book will illustrate to the defensive coach, through explanation and diagram, how the 53 Multiple Defense can readily adjust during actual game conditions to throttle an offensive opponent. Examples of these how-to-do-it defensive adjustments will be shown as follows:

1. How to adjust during game conditions to stop an explosive outside attack that is beating your defense at the flanks.
2. How to adjust during game conditions to stop a tough Power I or a Full-house T attack that is driving your interior lineman up into the bleachers.
3. How to adjust during game conditions, along the line of scrimmage, versus a team that is opening up gaping holes to allow quick offensive backs to "run to daylight" for large chunks of yardage.
4. How to adjust to game conditions to stop an option run or pass play that has befuddled your end and halfback.
5. How to adjust during game conditions to stop the belly option series that has gained a 2 on 1 advantage on your defensive end.
6. How to adjust during game conditions to stop a flanker or triple formation that features a run or pass play to the wide side of the field.

7. How to adjust during game conditions to stop an opponent with 4-1 on your 20 yard line, or on the goal line with one yard to go for the winning T.D.
8. How to adjust during game conditions to stop the long bomb with 20 seconds left in the game.
9. How to adjust during game conditions to stop a spread or unusual formation.
10. How to adjust during game conditions to stop an inside counter play that is eating up big yardage because an inside linebacker is getting faked out of position.

By making the proper defensive adjustment at the right time, the defensive team will eliminate errors. The end result is winning defensive football.

George H. Byers

Table of Contents

PART I

HOW TO ORGANIZE THE
53 MULTIPLE DEFENSE

1

Advantages and Objectives of the 53 Multiple Defense

AREA COVERAGES VERSUS RUN AND PASS

A sound defense must be prepared to cover all running and passing areas. We use the gap or man theory when planning our defenses versus the run. Our gap principle states that the Forcing Unit (defensive linemen and linebackers) must cover every offensive gap along the line of scrimmage, and our man principle states that the Forcing Unit must cover every offensive blocker along the line of scrimmage (Diagrams 1-1 and 1-2).

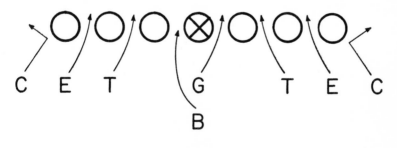

DIAGRAM 1-1
Gap Principle

It is possible to combine the gap and the man principle within the same defensive call. This type of combination call is sound as long as the Forcing Unit does not leave two offensive

19

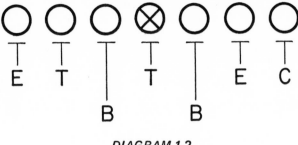

DIAGRAM 1-2
Man Principle

blockers or two offensive gaps, that are side by side, uncovered. An example could be a control call left and a pinching call right (Diagram 1-3).

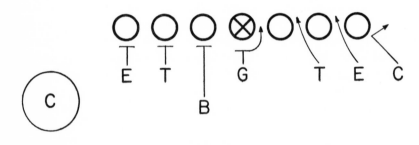

DIAGRAM 1-3
Combination Call

We double-check all of our defensive calls to be sure that our Forcing Unit follows the above rules of gap and man coverage. In our opinion, a defensive call that does not cover every gap or man is definitely weak versus an inside running attack.

We prefer to use zone pass coverage versus the passing game. Versus a tight offensive formation, we adjust into an Even alignment by dropping our middle guard into an inside linebacker position. This adjustment places two inside linebackers in excellent position to cover both inside hook zones, which is a definite weakness of the basic 53 defense. The corners cover the flat zones with our safety and defensive halfbacks covering the three deep zones (Diagram 1-4).

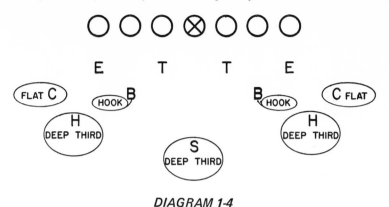

DIAGRAM 1-4

COVERAGE OF OFFENSIVE FORMATIONS

A sound defense must be prepared to adjust to any type of offensive formation from the most basic Tight-T to the most unusual formation. According to Ray Graves in his book entitled *Guide to Modern Football Defense,* the 53 Defense is the best in football in adjusting to spread or unusual formations. We definitely agree with Mr. Graves, and we believe that this is an excellent selling point for starting with the basic 53 alignment and then making adjustments from this alignment to meet various offensive game conditions. We have four simple rules of coverage which are applicable to all possible formations. These rules are applied as follows:

1. *Covering one split receiver.* The defensive halfback automatically moves out to cover a single split receiver to his side (Diagram 1-5).
2. *Covering two split receivers.* The defensive cornerman moves out automatically to cover a second split receiver to his side, such as a man in motion or a slotback (Diagram 1-5).
3. *Covering three split receivers.* The defensive end, corner, and the halfback move out to cover the three split receivers to the same side (Diagram 1-6).
4. *Covering an unusual formation.* The defensive ends, cornermen, and halfbacks should follow the previously mentioned rules. The middle guard, middle linebacker,

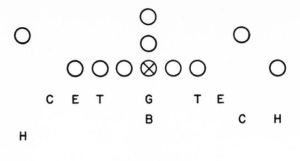

DIAGRAM 1-5

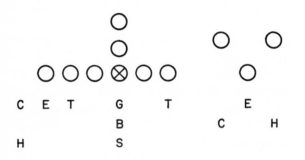

DIAGRAM 1-6

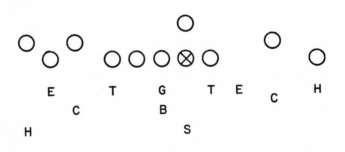

DIAGRAM 1-7

and the safety should position themselves automatically on the fourth man over from the end, or the middle of the offensive formation. The defensive tackles should always adjust themselves two men away from the middle guard. It is amazing how well our team can adjust to any type of unusual formation (Diagram 1-7).

COVERAGE OF OFFENSIVE PLAY ACTION

A sound defense must be prepared to adjust to all forms of offensive play action. We classify basic offensive play action in five categories: (1) run (inside and outside), (2) pass (drop back, screen, and draw), (3) play action pass, (4) roll- or sprint-out run or pass, and (5) reverse action run or pass (bootleg and throw back).

Versus an inside run our inside linebackers key through the uncovered linemen into the offensive backfield. Most teams will use specific types of blocking patterns which are directly associated with the offensive backfield action. Through our scouting reports, we determine which linemen and backs to key according to the expected offensive play action. For example, we key inside specifically for dive with man blocking, fullback or halfback slant with cross or trap blocking, Power I blast with the fullback leading as a trapper with a double team block inside, inside and outside belly series with man blocking, and cross buck type plays with man or trap blocking.

Versus an outside run our ends, corners, and halfbacks key for sweep, quick toss, and option. If both guards pull with the fullback leading, we key sweep. When the quarterback comes down the line of scrimmage with a trailing back, we key option, and when the tackle pulls out in front of the halfback on a quick toss play, we key toss. Specific coverages versus inside and outside running plays are covered in detail in Chapters 15 and 16.

If the quarterback drops straight back to pass, we expect our linebackers and safety men to read the uncovered linemen for pass blocking, and we expect our halfbacks and corners to read the release of the eligible receivers. We key for screen with our ends and corners, and for draw, with our middle tackle, inside linebackers and safety man, on every pass play. The coordinator of the Forcing and Containing Units versus the passing game is covered in detail in Chapter 11.

When the quarterback either rolls or sprints out with the football in a run or pass situation, we automatically key roll-out action all the way. We always key the near back away from the roll-out action for a possible throw back pass. This coverage is illustrated in Chapter 10.

If the offensive backfield fakes a definite running action, but the eligible receivers release down the field, we key pass all the way and the secondary men must yell "pass!" Our techniques and drills for keying and covering play action passes are shown in detail in Chapter 10.

If the entire flow of the backfield moves in one direction but the quarterback reverses back opposite this flow, we key bootleg. Corners and ends key through the near back to their side. If the near back leaves, they are drilled to look immediately for the quarterback to run a possible bootleg. This coverage is also covered in Chapter 10.

If the entire backfield flows one way, but the far back away from the flow reverses back into the opposite direction, we key reverse. Some teams will pull a guard or a tackle back to trap on a reverse play so we instruct our inside linebacker to key for a pulling lineman on reverse action. Reverse action coverages are illustrated in Chapter 10.

We firmly believe that it is vital for each defensive man to have a specific assignment versus each offensive play. In our opinion, one of the worst things a defensive coach can do is to place a defensive man in a position where he has to make a choice of one or two possible actions. Invariably, he will be forced by a well-drilled offensive unit to make the wrong decision, which could result in a "big play" for the offense. As a result, each of our eleven defensive men is given one specific assignment or coverage in meeting a specific offensive play. Through this approach, we believe that we eliminate possible mistakes or defensive errors.

ADJUSTING TO GAME SITUATIONS

A sound defense must be prepared to adjust to the following game situations: down and yardage, field position, and time left in the game.

We categorize down according to short, medium, or long yardage. Any down with 3 yards or less is considered short yardage, from 4 to 6 yards is medium yardage, and from 7 to more considered long yardage. We have a basic rule of thumb that we use as a guide in calling our defenses according to down and yardage. This rule states that 1-10, 2-8 or under, 3-6 or under, and 4-3 or under are considered running situation downs, and 1-15, 2-9 or more, 3-7 or more, and 4-4 or more are considered passing down situations. This basic rule is altered if our opponents' tendencies indicate a difference from our basic down and yardage rule. However, in most cases a typical team will fall into the above categories.

As a general rule, unless an opponent shows definite tendencies to go back to the short side of the field, we will favor our defenses to the wide side of the field. We believe that we need more men to cover two-thirds of the field than one-third of the field, as the offense has a great deal of running or passing area to exploit to the wide side. Also, we believe in the old cliché of using the sideline as an extra man.

As a general rule, we find that late in the game teams play conservatively when ahead and gamble when behind.

If a team is ahead of us late in the game, we feel that we must gamble on defense through attacking and blitzing maneuvers, our purpose being to force a fumble or to tackle the ball carrier behind the line of scrimmage for a loss of yardage. Through this strategy we can either retain possession of the ball or stop the opponent from making a first down. If we allow the opposition to march down the field making first downs, they will eat up time and we will be easily defeated.

If we are ahead late in the game, we must determine through scouting reports if our opponent has a two-minute offense. If the opposition has a good passing quarterback and receivers, we must be prepared to stop the sideline pass. A well-drilled passing team can march down the field throwing this pass by killing the clock after each reception with the receiver going out of bounds. To counter this passing threat, we place our secondary in our 5-deep alignment. The halfbacks must maintain a good outside relationship on the split receiver in position either to slap down the sideline pass or to tackle the receiver, not letting him get out of bounds to stop the clock. Our corner men are in an excellent position to support the halfback deep along with the safety man.

ADVANTAGES OF MOVING DEFENSIVE FOOTBALL

Below are listed several advantages of moving defensive football that we feel aptly illustrate why we believe that a small but quick man can compensate when meeting a large offensive blocker:

1. Moving defensive linemen and linebackers tend to confuse offensive blocking assignments, as a blocker is never sure which direction his opponent will take. The result is usually missed blocking assignments.

2. Moving linemen and linebackers can beat the blocker to the punch through quick movement on the snap of the ball. This is particularly true when the blocker hesitates when trying to anticipate the direction of our moving defensive men.

3. Moving linemen and linebackers present a difficult target for a blocker to make contact with, and, as a result, blockers usually lunge and become off balance in their blocking effort.

4. Moving linemen and linebackers can be directed into a specific area of offensive strength, meeting an anticipated offensive play with maximum strength at the point of attack according to the game situation or defensive game plan.

5. It is impossible for an offensive team to block our defensive men according to their original alignment as they will end up at a different spot after the snap of the ball. Many offensive teams still block according to either odd or even alignment, or according to a numbering system based upon the original line-up of the defense.

6. Our moving defensive men do not have to read first and then decide which area to defend against. They move to a specific area first, defend this area, and then react to the play. This relieves defensive linemen of the element of indecision, hesitation, and the chasing of faking backs in the wrong direction.

7. A moving defensive lineman, who is parallel to the line of scrimmage, has a big advantage over the offensive

blocker in body balance and position. He has the advantage of using his hands and reacting through natural movement. Maintaining good body balance and position while blocking a moving target places the blocker in an unnatural position and is one of the most difficult skills to master in the game of football.

ADJUSTING TO OFFENSIVE PERSONNEL OR TEAM STRENGTHS

We believe that we must adjust to and then shut off our opponent's number one and number two plays, or the "bread and butter" plays of the opposition. Through this defensive strategy we will force our opponent to run his third and fourth best plays. Many teams depend upon their bread and butter plays, and when they cannot run these plays successfully they are in dire trouble.

For example, most of our opponents, at the high school level, run from a split-end formation. From this formation they feature a passing attack to their split end and a sweep play to the tight end side. Thus, we would want to take away the sweep and the quick pass to the split end as the number one and number two plays.

We would take away the quick pass to the split end by dropping off our corner to double-cover this split receiver along with the halfback. To the tight end side, we would move our power corner up into position to attack the sweep from an outside position. Versus a split-end wing formation, we have had great success attacking the sweep from our odd alignment. The middle

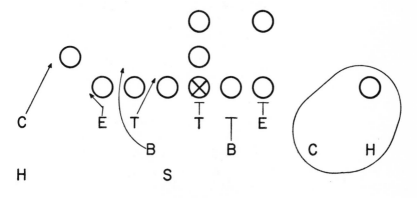

DIAGRAM 1-8

guard moves back into an inside linebacker position and then attacks the tackle gap on sweep action. With our power corner attacking from the outside and our linebacker from the inside, we prevent the sweep from turning the corner, forcing the ball carrier deep and to the outside for a loss in yardage (Diagram 1-8).

Our Forcing Unit has the flexibility to adjust into several front alignments. We are convinced that a multiple defensive system with the flexibility to design tailor-made defensive calls to counter specific modern offensive plays is a must in modern defensive football. These front alignments, which vary according to the anticipated offensive play action or the offensive formation, are covered in detail in Chapters 15 to 17.

DEFENSIVE FOOTBALL THAT IS OFFENSIVE-MINDED

We are convinced that defensive teams should be offensive-minded, because there are more ways to score on defense than offense. It is possible to score on defense as follows: (1) to recover a fumble over the goal line, (2) to pick up a fumbled ball—in high school—to score, (3) to block a punt for a touchdown, (4) to intercept a pass for a touchdown, (5) to return a punt or kick off for a touchdown, and (6) to force a safety. Therefore, in our opinion, defensive teams should take advantage of this opportunity to score. This can be done through "attacking defensive football."

Attacking defensive teams will put much pressure on the offense. For example, pressure on the quarterback can force him to throw that bad pass for an easy interception; pressure on the punter can force a blocked punt for a possible score; pressure on the ball carrier, through gang tackling, can result in a fumble and a possible score; and pressure on the offense can result in a safety.

HITTING DEFENSIVE FOOTBALL

We believe that "hitting" ability is the basis for an aggressive defense that features gang tackling plus "great" hitting technique. It is important, to our defensive thinking, that we install pride within our defensive unit through the feeling that we can out-hit any team that we play against, and our coaching staff works hard to motivate our men in this direction. Our hitting drills and techniques are covered in detail in Chapters 12 to 14.

DEVELOPING DESIRE, PRIDE, AND CONFIDENCE

We are convinced that the most important factor in developing an outstanding defensive unit is the development of desire, pride, and confidence within this unit. A defensive unit that is imbued with these fine attributes will be made up of hitting, hustling, and courageous players who will never give up or be satisfied unless they have given their greatest performance, every game, to help their team win a great victory. In our opinion, defense is unique in that men just naturally get fired-up or excited about defense, as natural football players love contact. We try to take advantage of this inner feeling or longing for contact to develop great enthusiasm and pride within the defensive unit.

GOAL OF THE 53 MULTIPLE DEFENSE

The ultimate goal of our multiple defense, through the attainment of our objectives, is to prevent our opponent from scoring, and then either to score on defense or to provide our offensive team with excellent field position to score a touchdown.

2

Selecting and Utilizing Personnel for the 53 Multiple Defense

We believe that every member of the Multiple 53 defensive unit must possess quickness and aggressiveness. These two characteristics are a must. Therefore, we select our quickest and most aggressive eleven men to play on our defensive unit, and we design our defensive drills to develop these qualities that are so vital in the development of outstanding defensive players. However, each of our individual defensive positions requires a specific type of athlete or football player. The following information will explain in detail the necessary physical requirements of each position.

SELECTION AND UTILIZATION OF DEFENSIVE ENDS

The number one requirement for our defensive ends is quickness. Quickness is imperative because our defensive ends must be able to contain the quarterback on roll-out or sprint-out, run or pass plays and on the quarterback option run, keep, or pitch. Also, on occasion, defensive ends must have the quickness to cover the flat or swing areas in a passing situation. Ideally, we like rangy men who are six feet tall or better, as this type is difficult to pass over. This is particularly true when the quarterback attempts to throw the quick look-in pass to a split end. If we can get size and weight along with quickness this, of course, is the ideal situation. When we go into our tight defensive front alignments, the defensive ends move inside over the offensive tackle to the tight end side, or over the offensive guard to the split end side. Thus, additional size and weight helps when we move into these tight front alignments. However, since our defensive system is basically a moving defense, we depend more upon quickness and fast reaction than on size and strength to counter offensive play action. Again, we select our quickest defensive linemen to play defensive end.

SELECTION AND UTILIZATION OF DEFENSIVE TACKLES

The number one requirement of our defensive tackles is quickness along with size and strength. We need size and strength at this position because our tackles must be strong enough to shut off the inside running game. Defensive tackles do not have to be as quick as defensive ends, as their movement is limited to a small area. On occasion, we ask our tackles to be physically strong enough to control an offensive lineman in a man-on-man situation through the use of a control charge. Again, we select our biggest and strongest linemen to play defensive tackle.

SELECTION AND UTILIZATION OF
MIDDLE GUARD AND MIDDLE BACKER

The middle guard and middle linebacker must be two of the best athletes on the team. This is particularly true when running the basic 53 defense without multiple variations.

We select our most athletic lineman with size and quickness to be our middle guard. This man must be our best defensive lineman, as he must be able to control the center and then slide into either gap to stop an offensive play up the middle. A quick and alert middle guard who is on the move can play havoc with an offensive center and offensive guard. We like to get size and range if we can get it. However, quickness and agility are a must and we will sacrifice size for quickness if we cannot find one of our larger lineman with these physical characteristics. A tall middle guard can key the quarterback on quick passes over the middle and, when he times it right, he can get up into the air to block this type of pass. Size is not a necessity, as a small man with great quickness and agility can excel at this position—at the high school level.

The middle linebacker must be the best linebacker-type athlete on the team. This man must have outstanding quickness, agility and aggressiveness, as well as the natural instinct to "smell out" the ball carrier. He must be at the right place at the right time. It also takes outstanding lateral movement to play this position, as the middle linebacker must be able to cover a defensive area from tackle to tackle, without the support of a second inside linebacker. This man is generally one of the defensive captains, and he must be capable of making the "big" play so that his teammates will respect him. Such a man can be of tremendous value to the defensive unit, as he can inspire his teammates to great heights.

When we have had two outstanding men to fill the middle guard and middle linebacker positions, the basic 53 was a very effective defense. However, as we progressed with our 53 defense—at the high school level—we found that we had to adjust our basic defense to meet new offensive trends. As a result, we had to go to multiple variations to make better utilization of our personnel. As we experimented with new adjustments, we found that the middle guard type of football player was also well-suited to play an inside linebacker position, as he had the natural quickness and agility to fill this position. Also, the middle guard had more size than a typical high school linebacker, and we could use this additional size and strength to good advantage by placing this man at a linebacker position to the strong side of the offensive formation. Thus, we could get a bigger and stronger man opposite a larger and stronger offensive tackle. This gave us a two inside linebacker system, with the middle linebacker aligned to the split end or weak side of the offensive formation. Thus, we could use the quickness and speed of the middle linebacker to pass coverage to the split end side to great advantage in passing situations.

During the years when we have not had two outstanding men to fill these positions, we have used a two inside linebacker system almost exclusively. We identify our inside backers as the "Power" and "Quick" linebackers. The Power Backer always aligns to the tight end side or strong side of the offensive formation, and the Quick Backer always aligns to the split-end or weak side of the offensive formation. This second inside linebacker, as compared to the single middle linebacker, is of great assistance in covering the defensive area inside from tackle to tackle, as the two inside backers only have to cover half as much ground as a middle linebacker. Through this approach the inside linebackers do not have to be quite as gifted, physically, as a middle linebacker. However, when we employ the two inside linebacker system our Power Backer, on occasion, is used as a middle guard, as there are game situations that call for the 53 alignment as the best possible defensive call.

Ideally, within our multiple defensive system of play, we prefer to have an outstanding defensive lineman who can double as a middle guard or a power linebacker. As an inside linebacker, he can align as a "54 Okie" or a 62 inside linebacker, or he can align on the outside shoulder of the tight end on a Pro-61 type of defensive call. In addition, our middle linebacker can align in this position on a 53 or a Pro-61 type call, or he can align in an inside, quick linebacker position as an "Okie 54" or a 62 inside linebacker. With such flexibility as this, we can "jump" our middle guard and middle linebacker around into several front alignments, which is a great advantage in adjusting to various offensive game conditions. Our system for calling these alignments and then moving into them is very simple and is explained in detail in Chapter 3.

SELECTION AND UTILIZATION OF
DEFENSIVE CORNER MEN

The key to our flexible Multiple 53 Defense is the play of our defensive corners in conjunction with the play of our middle guard and middle linebacker. This is true, as our corner men can be utilized as defensive ends, inside linebackers, outside linebackers, or deep secondary men.

When we first began with our 53 Defense, we utilized our corners strictly as outside linebackers. However, as offensive teams began to use more split end flanker Pro-type formations, we had to make definite adjustments with our defensive corners. This was true because we found that we had a glaring weakness in the seam area, between the defensive halfback and safety, to the split end or flanker side (Diagram 2-1). Our 3-deep secondary was definitely weakened in this seam area. Thus, we adjusted to this weakness by dropping our corners back into these seam areas in a definite passing situation. This adjustment placed our secondary in either a 4-deep or a 5-deep secondary, depending upon whether we dropped just one or both of our corners.

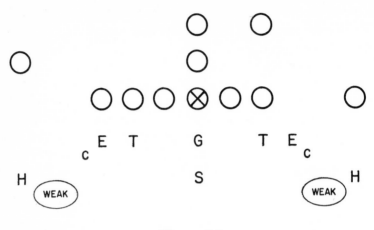

Diagram 2-1

Also, many teams were beginning to run power sweep plays to the tight end or strong side of the offensive formation. To counter this sweep threat, we felt that we needed quick and tough outside support to immediately force the sweep and prevent the sweep from turning the corner. We adjusted to this situation by using an "even" front alignment, with our outside corner man moving up to the line of scrimmage in a wide tackle six end alignment. This alignment placed the corner in an ideal position from which to force the sweep deep and to the outside.

As we made these adjustments we found that we were using the "monster" principles used in the single monster defense. So we began to call our corner men monsters and we utilized them exactly as monster men are used within the single monster defense. However, in our opinion, we have an advantage over the single monster defense in that we have two monsters within a balanced defense, rather than just one monster within an over-shifted or unbalanced defense, such as the single monster defense.

Because of the flexibility in the play of our corner monster men, they must possess specific abilities such as speed, quickness, agility, aggressiveness, and the ability to play pass defense. They should have enough size and range to play "run tough" as defensive ends or outside linebackers with enough speed to cover the deep pass. These monster men must possess the same qualities as a single monster man used in the single monster defense. The better athletes on the squad should be the prime prospects for this position. One approach is to select two of the most aggressive defensive backs with good speed to play the position. Such a man has the aggressiveness to contain the running game and the speed to cover the deep pass. It is possible—at the high school level—to get by with a smaller monster as long as he is extremely quick and aggressive and loves contact. Tight ends and fullbacks with good hands are also good prospects for this position, as they normally possess the additional size to go along with the other attributes mentioned as necessary for corner monster men.

We have found that it is an advantage to have a bigger and stronger corner-type to the tight end or the strong side of the offensive formation, and a quicker and faster man or corner to the split end side in position to help double cover the split end. Thus, we recommend the use of a Power Corner and a Quick Corner. The Quick Corner would always align to the weak side or split end side of the offensive formation. He would have the speed of a fourth defensive back and he would not have to be as big as the Power Corner. From this position, he could use his speed and pass defense ability to the open or split end side of the formation. The Power Corner would always align to the strong side or tight end side of the offensive formation. He would be bigger and stronger than the Quick Monster, as his primary responsibility would be to contain the running game to the strong side or tight side of the line. However, the Power Corner would have enough speed to cover a deep pass or play the tight end or fullback on a man-to-man basis.

The selection of the type of corner monster man that is needed will depend upon the style of offensive football played by opponents. When playing against tight formation running type teams, the power type corner that can play the outside as a defensive end or linebacker would be ideal. However, when defensing split formation teams that feature the passing game, the quick monster type is better suited to covering the passing game.

Ideally, it is best to select two outstanding athletes, as corners, who have the ability to play both the pass and the run equally well. Such men possess the flexibility to adjust to varied offensive game situations, which is necessary when meeting flexible offensive teams. In the final analysis the coach's selection of his corner monsters will depend upon the personnel available, his style of defense, and the style of offensive football played by his opponents.

SELECTION AND UTILIZATION OF
DEFENSIVE HALFBACKS

Defensive halfbacks must be good "ball hawks," good tacklers, and possess good natural reaction, quickness, and speed. A good defensive halfback seems to have the natural instinct to be at the right place at the right time. The selection of the defensive halfback again will depend upon the style of offensive football played by opposing offensive teams. If opponents feature a passing game with split receivers, the defensive halfbacks will have to have good speed and pass defense ability. If opponents use tight formations stressing a running attack, the defensive halfbacks must be good tacklers in order to rotate up and help contain the running game. Ideally, the coach should strive to find flexible athletes who can play both the run and pass equally well, as men of this caliber are capable of adjusting to different opponents and various game situations.

SELECTION AND UTILIZATION OF
DEFENSIVE SAFETY

The defensive safety, along with the corner monsters, should be one of the best athletes on the team. He must possess speed, aggressiveness and leadership ability, and he must be a good ball hawk. He must have the knack of being at the right place at the right time in the same manner as the halfback. The safety is used to make secondary calls; therefore, intelligence and leadership qualities are important from this standpoint. He is used for rotation in covering the deep outside zones, so good speed is a priority. Occasionally we like to call a safety blitz, so aggressiveness and tackling ability are important considerations. Also, the safety is a last resort man if an offensive back breaks into the open en route to a touchdown so that, again, speed and tackling ability play an important role in the position of safety. Ideally, size and range are great assets to the safety man.

3

Setting Up Defensive Alignment and Calls

BASIC 53 ALIGNMENT

Originally we began with a 53 Corner defensive alignment as a basic alignment. From this alignment, we used both a pinching and a control defensive charge. We would pinch into the inside gaps on a running down and drop off into a control charge on a passing down. (Diagrams 3-1 and 3-2).

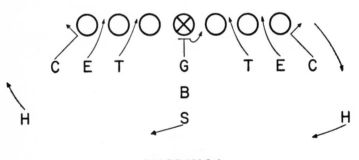

DIAGRAM 3-1
Pinch Charge

These defenses were borrowed from my father, Herman Byers. Herman Byers spent 40 years coaching high school football in the state of Indiana. His last 26 years of coaching (he is now retired) were spent as head coach at Reitz High in Evansville,

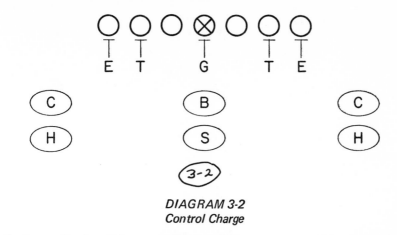

DIAGRAM 3-2
Control Charge

Indiana. During this span of years his teams won 188 games, lost 51, and tied 14. He coached 8 undefeated teams, won 14 city championships, 13 conference championships, and won 6 mythical state championships.

During the early 1960's high school football teams were running quick-hitting T formation plays from tight offensive formations. Herman Byers stymied this offensive attack with his original 53 pinching defense. In fact, this defense was so devastating that his 1961 defensive team held his opponents scoreless—an unprecedented feat and record for high school football teams in the state of Indiana.

We used the basic 53 pinching and control defenses at Irvington High during our first year, 1964, in the Mission Valley Athletic League in Fremont, California, and we led our league in team defense. This defense was murder against an inside running attack. However, we found that many of our opponents were beginning to use split-end and flanker formations, and the quarterback roll-out run or pass option was becoming very popular. We therefore had to make definite adjustments from our basic 53 defense to cover split-end formations and the roll-out play.

Our defensive halfback was forced to move out from his tight alignment to cover a split receiver at a distance of 8 to 12 yards. He was forced to drop back into his deep third zone and play the split receiver for a pass on every down. Another predicament prevailed. Although we always selected one of our fastest backs to play safety, the distance he would have to rotate from his middle safety zone to cover the split receiver would be an impossible task to ask of a high school player. Thus, we could not get our normal rotation with the halfback containing the run outside or flat pass, and the safety rotating to his deep third zone to side of flow as shown in Diagram 3-1.

To compensate for this lack of rotation, the defensive corner contained an outside run or covered the flat pass with the end in position to contain the quarterback on roll-out action. A control or slant technique placed our defensive end in an ideal position to execute these outside assignments.

From our 53 defense, we used a control charge to the flanker side and a pinching charge to the back side. We were forced to overshift our middle linebacker to the strong side of the offensive formation. This adjustment took care of the outside corner area in fine fashion. However, this adjustment left a hole over the middle which was weak versus inside counter or quick hitting fullback dives (Diagram 3-3).

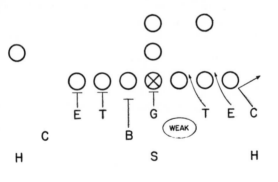

DIAGRAM 3-3

About this time the 52 Slanting Defense was beginning to become popular. We could see a definite advantage that this defensive alignment offered in that we could cover the outside game with a "slant" technique and still cover the holes up the middle with two inside linebackers. Thus, we adjusted our middle guard back into a power linebacker position and overshifted our line to the side of formation strength (Diagram 3-4).

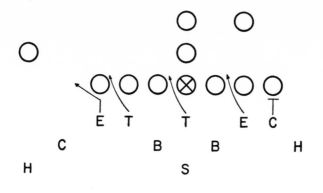

DIAGRAM 3-4

Moreover, the sweep play to the flanker side and the quick passing game to the split end, such as the look-in, sideline, and curl patterns, became very popular. We adjusted to the sweep play by moving our power corner up to the line of scrimmage in a wide tackle, six-end defensive alignment. From this position, the corner was in an ideal position to put quick and tough pressure on the lead blocker to force the ball carrier deep and wide towards the sidelines. When we moved the corner up, we adjusted into an even alignment which placed our power linebacker in an excellent position to support the corner outside versus sweep (Diagram 3-5).

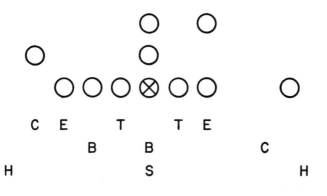

DIAGRAM 3-5

We adjust to the quick passing attack to the split end by dropping off our quick corner in position to help double cover the split end with the defensive halfback (Diagram 3-5).

We also found a need to adjust into other defensive alignments because of the offensive strengths or weaknesses of our opponent, or because of the physical strengths or weaknesses of our defensive personnel during a specific season. All of these various alignments and the reasons for these alignments will be explained and illustrated later in this chapter under Adjusted Defensive Alignments.

DEFENSIVE CALL SYSTEM

The purpose of each defensive call is to tell every man on our defensive unit where to align and which technique or coverage to execute. Because our Forcing Unit coordinates with our Contain Unit, we use a single defensive call which automatically tells both units where to align and which technique or coverage to employ.

The first part of each defensive call tells the Forcing Unit where to align. The defensive quarterback merely calls out any of the possible defensive front alignments, shown in Diagrams 3-17 to 4-4. The most basic call would be a simple "odd" or "even" call. An odd or even call automatically tells our linemen to align in a basic odd or even alignment. When we want to vary either basic alignment, we give an additional call that will identify the change. Examples would be an Even-Tight, which tells our interior linemen and corners to move into a tight alignment; Inside call such as an Even-Inside, which tells our corners to move into an Inside attacking position; and a Double call which tells our middle guard and middle linebacker to move into a Double position with the middle guard and the middle linebacker stacked over the offensive center in double fashion.

The second part of the defensive call tells our Forcing Unit which technique to use. Diagram 3-6 illustrates an Even-Slant-Right call. "Slant" tells our Forcing Unit which technique to use and "Right" tells them the direction of the charge.

Since our secondary coverage must complement the technique used by our linemen, this "technique" call for the linemen also tells our secondary men where to align and which coverage and technique to use. To the slanting side our corner knows that he automatically aligns in a basic "walk-away" position and that it is his job to either cover the flat or help contain the outside run. The back side, or pinching corner, knows that he automatically aligns in a tight pinching position and uses a pinching technique to his side to contain an outside running play. As can be seen in Diagram 3-6, this illustration clearly shows how our corners complement the play of both the Forcing Unit and the Containing Unit.

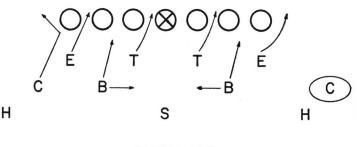

DIAGRAM 3-6
Even-Slant Right

Other examples of technique calls would be pinch, control, and loop left or right. When we want to use an attack technique, we call out the name of the area we plan to attack. We always attack one of the eight offensive gaps, and we have these gaps named as indicated in Diagram 3-7. Center gaps are between the guards and center, guard gaps are between the guards and tackles, tackle gaps are between the tackles and tight ends, and the end gaps are located just outside the tight ends.

DIAGRAM 3-7

In most instances the linebackers automatically attack the specifically called gaps on an "attack" call. However, we do like to mix up our attack plans by attacking our corners or safety man. We will attack our corners into the Tackle Gap on an inside call, and into the end outside area on an End Attack call, and we can call a "Safety Blitz" into any of the named inside gaps. For example, if we wanted to attack the Tackle Gap we could call an Even-Tight-Tackle Gap (linebacker attack), Odd-Inside-Tackle Gap (corner attack), Odd-Tackle Gap (linebacker attack, or an Even-Tight-Safety-Tackle Gap. As can be seen, the Safety-Tackle Gap call is identical to the other calls, with the term safety inserted before the Tackle Gap call to indicate that the safety would attack. In this situation the linebackers know that they must align in their basic positions away from the designated attack call, and the Forcing Unit carries out their basic attack techniques. Thus, the only change in a Safety-Tackle Gap call is that the safety man is attacking the side of the call rather than the linebacker (Diagrams 3-8 to 3-11).

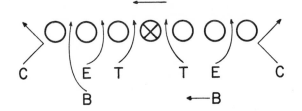

DIAGRAM 3-8
Even-Tight-Tackle Gap

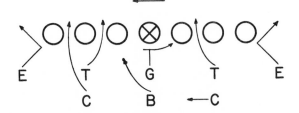

DIAGRAM 3-9
Odd-Inside-Double Tackle Gap

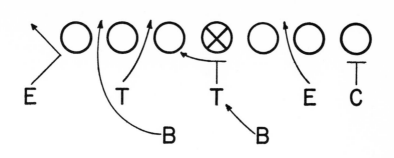

DIAGRAM 3-10
Odd-Tackle Gap

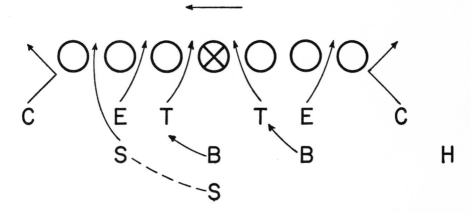

DIAGRAM 3-11
Even-Tight-Safety-Tackle
Gap-Left

Other examples of possible calls when anticipating a run would be an Odd-Slant-Right or an Even-End Attack. We could use these types of calls to get better outside support into the outside End Attack area (Diagrams 3-12 and 3-13)

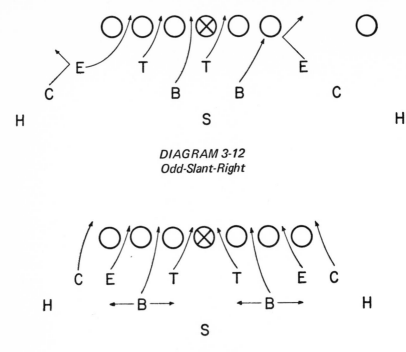

DIAGRAM 3-12
Odd-Slant-Right

DIAGRAM 3-13
Even-End Attack

In most instances we do not have to give an additional call for the secondary. However, on occasion we do use more than one secondary coverage in conjunction with a single defensive call. When we mix up this coverage our safety man will give a separate call. In this situation, the various secondary calls and coverages used in conjunction with a single front line call will still complement the play of the Forcing Unit. This is a must, as we strongly believe that that these separate units must function as one unit. An example of an additional call given by the safety man could be illustrated from an Odd-Control-Pass Defense call. On this call our linemen automatically use a Control charge and our secondary uses a basic 5-deep zone pass defense coverage. If we wanted a "change-up" in our secondary coverage from a zone to double coverage, our safety man could give a Double Right-Zone Left call. This would tell our halfback and corner to the right side to double-cover the split end, with the rest of the secondary using zone pass coverage. The entire call in this case would be a first call of Odd-Control-Pass Defense with a second call of Double Right-Zone Left (Diagram 3-14).

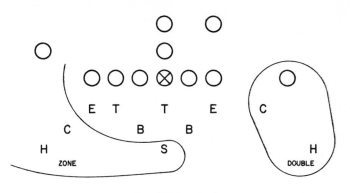

DIAGRAM 3-14
Double Right-Zone Left

In the past we have used numbers and code words in calling defenses. However, we have found that with high school players numbers and code words sometimes become confusing. As a result, we have gone to descriptive terms. Each descriptive term, by name, specifically tells each defensive man what to do. For example, "Slant-Right" actually tells our linemen specifically, by name, what to do, and "Double-Right" tells our corner and halfback specifically, by name, what to do. When we attack, our descriptive term such as "Center-Gap" actually tells our linebacker exactly where to go when attacking. This method of calling defenses has simplified our system tremendously, as our men do not have to memorize what numbers or code words mean.

ADJUSTED DEFENSIVE
ALIGNMENTS

Our basic alignment versus the run is our original 53 alignment. However, as we adjusted this defensive front, we found that we could easily design many defensive variations through our simple but flexible call system. Through this approach, we can actually duplicate any of the basic defensive alignments in football, as described in the following diagrams.

Odd-Double

We call our basic 53 defense an Odd-Double. "Odd" tells the defensive ends and tackles to align in a basic odd front alignment, and "Double" tells the Middle Guard and Middle Linebacker to align in "Double Fashion" over the offensive center. The corners align 1½ yards in width and depth, in a pinching position from the offensive tight end, and the secondary aligns in the traditional 3-deep alignment. This alignment is used primarily as a Pinching Defense, as previously illustrated in Diagram 3-1. From this basic alignment, we can also use a Control Defense with the corners dropped off 4 yards in width and depth in their basic corner positions (Diagram 3-2).

Odd-Double-Inside

The Odd-Double call automatically tells our Forcing Unit where to align, as previously shown, and the Inside call tells the defensive corners to move into an inside position directly behind the defensive tackles. The secondary aligns in their basic 3-deep alignment. However, on a running down we can cheat our defensive halfbacks up to 5 yards so they are in good position to help contain the outside End Gap area in a hurry.

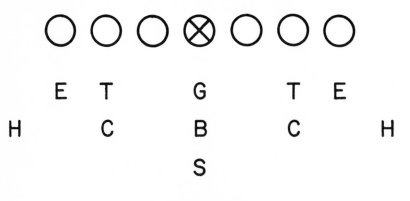

DIAGRAM 3-15
Odd-Double-Inside

This is an excellent attacking defense, as we can get an over-load effect at the Tackle-Gap area and still get excellent inside support from a middle linebacker. This defense is very difficult to run against with an inside running attack (Diagram 3-15).

Odd

When we first began using Slanting Defenses, we shifted to an Odd alignment with our middle guard moving into a Power Linebacker position. This adjustment gave our defense a 52 defensive look.

"Odd" tells the defensive tackles and the defensive end away from the strength of the offensive formation to overshift one man to this side of offensive strength. The Power Corner moves up on the outside shoulder of the tight end to the weak side, and the Quick Corner aligns in a basic corner position to the strong side. This corner adjustment places our bigger and stronger corner on the line of scrimmage with our smaller quick corner playing his basic corner position. The defensive end to the side of formation strength will remain in his basic Odd alignment on the outside shoulder of the tight end.

Versus a tight formation, we like to squirm our defensive halfback to the weak side up into a corner position, with our defensive safety man also sliding to the weak side and aligning over the offensive guard (Diagram 3-16).

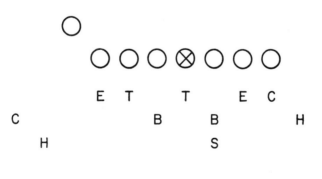

DIAGRAM 3-16
Odd

We like to Attack the Tackle-Gap from this alignment as we can get an over-load effect into this area.

Odd-Inside

We use this alignment more against split-end teams. This is true because we can double-cover the split end with our Quick Corner and defensive halfback and still get three inside line-backers. This gives our defensive front a 53 look versus the inside running game. We can call an Odd-Power-Inside with the Power Corner aligned in an inside linebacker position, or an Odd-Quick-Inside with the Quick Corner aligned in an inside linebacker position. The two inside linebackers merely overshift to the side away from the Inside call.

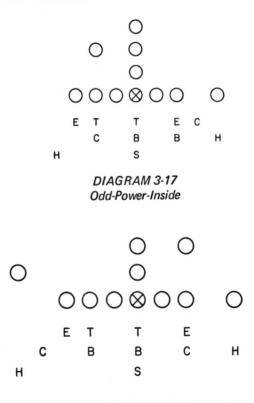

DIAGRAM 3-17
Odd-Power-Inside

DIAGRAM 3-18
Odd-Quick-Inside

We prefer to make the Inside call to the short side of the field or away from formation strength. Through this approach, we always get a corner aligned in the basic corner (walk-away) position in excellent position to defend against the pass or outside option or roll-out type plays. This alignment is used as an Attacking Defense for the same reasons as described for the Odd-Double-Inside defense (Diagrams 3-17 and 3-18).

Odd-Double-Tight

"Odd-Double" tells the Forcing Unit where to align, and the additional term "tight" tells the defensive tackles, ends, and corners to move one man down to the inside. The corners align on the outside shoulder of the tight ends. This gives the defense a 71 look (Diagram 3-19).

This is an excellent defense versus a tough inside running game. If the defense has an outstanding middle guard and middle linebacker, they are in business. With every offensive blocker covered along the line of scrimmage it is very difficult to block the middle linebacker. As a result, he is free to roam behind the defensive line to make easy tackles. The middle guard covers the back side gap away from the flow checking for possible counter plays to the inside.

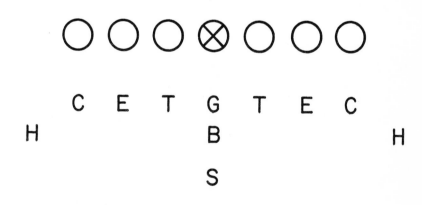

DIAGRAM 3-19
Odd-Double-Tight

Even

We prefer to use this alignment as our basic alignment in a definite passing situation. This is true because we can get two inside linebackers in position to cover the hook zones with two corner men in position to cover the two flat zones.

"Even" tells our defensive tackles to align head-up over the offensive guards, and the defensive ends to align head-up over the tight ends. The Power linebacker aligns two yards off the line of scrimmage head-up over the offensive tackle to the side of formation strength, and the Quick linebacker aligns in this same basic position to the weak side of the offensive formation. The corner men align in their basic corner position, which is four yards in depth and width from the tight end. The secondary aligns in the basic 3-deep alignment with the halfbacks 2 yards outside of the tight ends and 8 yards in depth. The safety is 12 yards deep and aligned directly over the offensive center. This gives our defense a 44 look, which is used in a definite passing situation (Diagram 3-20).

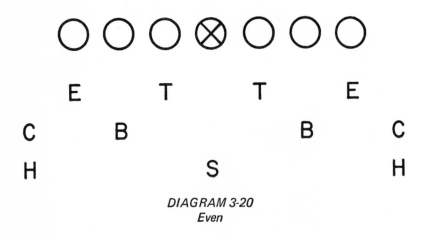

DIAGRAM 3-20
Even

Even-Attack

"Even" tells the Forcing Unit where to align and "Attack" tells the corner men to move up into a wide tackle, six end alignment. From this defensive position, the corners are in an ideal position to attack or contain the outside running game. This gives our defense a 62 look (Diagram 3-21).

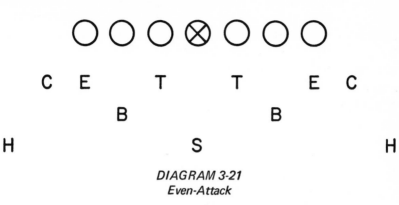

DIAGRAM 3-21
Even-Attack

Even-Split

"Even" tells the Forcing Unit where to align; "Split" tells the defensive tackles to move to the outside shoulder of the offensive guards, and the two inside linebackers to move into the Center-Gaps. We attack on a Split call so that the corners automatically move up into an attacking position. The secondary aligns in a 3-deep. This defense gives us an over-load effect at the Center-Gaps, which affords excellent attacking opportunities into this area (Diagram 3-22).

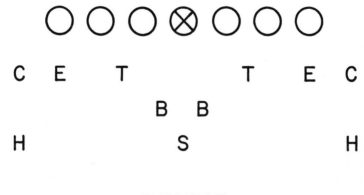

DIAGRAM 3-22
Even-Split

Even-Inside

"Even" tells the Forcing Unit where to align and "Inside" tells the corner men to move into an inside position directly behind the defensive end. On this call, the two inside linebackers automatically stack in an attacking position directly behind the defensive tackles. The secondary aligns in a basic 3-deep alignment. This gives our defense a 44 stacked look. This is an excellent attacking defense for small but quick and aggressive linemen and linebackers, as this type of attack plan can create a great deal of confusion for offensive blockers (Diagram 3-23).

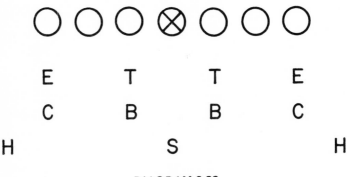

DIAGRAM 3-23
Even-Inside

Even-Tight

"Even" tells the Forcing Unit where to align and "Tight" tells the tackles, ends, and corners to move down one man to the inside. The tackles align on the inside shoulder of the offensive guards. The two inside linebackers move into a stacked position behind the defensive tackles. The corners automatically align on the outside shoulder of the tight ends and the secondary aligns in their 3-deep. This defense gives us an over-load effect at either the Guard-Gaps or Tackle-Gaps, which affords the Forcing Unit excellent attacking opportunities into these areas (Diagram 3-24). This alignment gives us a Tight 62 look.

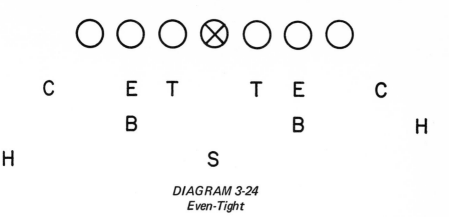

DIAGRAM 3-24
Even-Tight

Even-Tight-Pro

"Even-Tight" tells our Forcing Unit where to align and "Pro" tells the Power Linebacker to align on the outside shoulder to the tight end at the side of formation strength. Versus a tight line, the Power Corner will align on the outside shoulder of the tight end to the weak side of the offensive formation and the Quick Corner will align in a basic corner position to the side of offensive strength. Again, in this situation we like to squirm the secondary with the halfback and safety favoring the weak side, as previously illustrated.

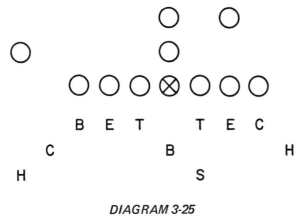

DIAGRAM 3-25
Even-Tight-Pro

DIAGRAM 3-26
Even-Tight-Goal-Line

This is an excellent defense when the interior linemen are physically big and strong, as they can align head-up and use a control charge to control the offensive blocker. With an outstanding middle linebacker in position to roam behind a strong defensive line this can be a devastating defense (Diagram 3-25).

Even-Tight-Goal Line

"Even-Tight" tells the forcing Unit and Corners where to align and "Goal line" tells the two inside linebackers to move into a linebacker position on the inside shoulder of the tight end and the safety to move into a middle linebacker position. The defensive halfbacks move up into defensive corner positions. This defense is used on the goal line and in short-yardage situations. This alignment gives us a 65 look (Diagram 3-26).

PART II

HOW TO COORDINATE THE 53 MULTIPLE FORCING UNIT

4

Coordinating the 53 Multiple Forcing Unit

FUNDAMENTALS FOR COORDINATING THE FORCING UNIT

The basic Forcing Unit consists of six men, namely, the two defensive ends, two defensive tackles, the middle guard, and the middle linebacker. Although the defensive corner men are considered a part of the "Containing Unit" or secondary, they also become an important part of the Forcing Unit when we employ our 8-Man front alignments.

The defensive Forcing Unit must coordinate together as a cohesive group. Initially, they will align according to the defensive call. From this alignment, the Forcing Unit must key the offensive formation and the placement of the offensive backs and ends. There are definite strengths and weaknesses within every offensive formation, according to the placement of the offensive ends and backs. The Forcing Unit must be aware of these strengths and weaknesses so that they can anticipate the most logical offensive plays to be run by our opponent. After identifying the offensive formation, such as Tight-T, the Forcing Unit is instructed to call out the name of this formation. The strengths and weaknesses of offensive formations are covered in detail in Chapters 15 to 17.

We believe that we must key every offensive formation from both an inside and an outside position. This gives the Forcing Unit an excellent overall birds's-eye view of the entire offense.

The inside linebackers and the middle guard are responsible for keying from an inside position. They must key through the uncovered linemen, guards or tackles, into the "near" back and quarterback. The near back is either the halfback or the fullback, according to which back is set nearest to them. They must diagnose the type of movement of the uncovered lineman through to the movement or the flow of the near back and quarterback. This movement will key the offensive play action. On key, the Forcing Unit must call out the name of the offensive play action. Every man on the Forcing Unit has a specific assignment according to the offensive play action, and, upon recognition of this play action, each man executes his specific assignments. These specific keys according to the offensive play action are covered in detail in Chapters 15 to 17.

The defensive ends and corners key from an outside position. They key through the tight end to the near back and quarterback. Again, on key, the ends and corners diagnose the movement of their keys and then call out the name of the offensive play action. Through our specific keys, the ends and corners can easily key run or pass and then react accordingly to the type of play action and the called coverage. These keys and coverages are covered in detail in Chapters 15 to 17.

FIVE BASIC TECHNIQUES AND FOUR RESPONSIBILITIES FOR THE FORCING UNIT

The entire Forcing Unit keys on the move, and they can execute one of five basic techniques according to the defensive call. These techniques are the Pinch, Attack, Slant, Loop, and Control techniques. As they execute each technique, they have four basic responsibilities. First, they must follow either our Gap or Man principle of area coverage along the line of scrimmage. Next, according to the called offensive play action, they must execute their specific assignments by picking up an assigned offensive back to the side of flow. Through this approach our defense gains the following advantages: (1) By assigning specific defensive men to take specific offensive men on a man-to-man basis, they take their assigned back and do not get faked out of position by taking the wrong back. (2) Defensive men do not get caught in a 2 on 1 option situation, such as a belly option, as we always assign a specific man to take the quarterback and the pitch men. (3) We can design "tailor made" defensive plays from week to week to stop specific offensive plays.

The third responsibility involves back side coverages. The back side end or corner away from flow must key for a possible outside reverse, bootleg, or throw-back pass. If the end is aligned on the outside shoulder of the tight end, he is responsible for back side containment. If the end pinches or attacks to his inside, the corner is responsible for back side containment.

The back side "contain" man keys through the tight end to the near back and quarterback. If the near back leaves with the flow, he automatically keys the quarterback for "Bootleg" and the tight end blocking down to his inside for a Reverse play. If either of these plays develop, he must contain them to his inside. If there is no Bootleg or Reverse, the contain man will then pursue back over the short middle or back into the outside deep third zone according to the called coverage. If the near back swings back opposite the flow of the quarterback, the contain man must cover him short for a possible throw-back pass.

The back side linebacker or an Inside corner linebacker, away from flow, must always check for an inside counter play. With flow away, they automatically become a middle linebacker.

And lastly, after it has been determined that the offensive play is definitely away from their assigned area of coverage, the entire Forcing Unit must pursue the football following the proper lines of pursuit.

The following chapters will explain how we coordinate the Forcing Unit when executing our five basic techniques. However, we will not cover specific keys or assignments according to offensive play action. This detailed information will be covered separately in Part V, which covers team defensive adjustments versus offensive play action.

5

Coordinating the Pinch and
Attack Techniques

COORDINATED PINCH TECHNIQUES

The purpose of the Pinch technique is to seal off the inside gaps. We prefer to use either the Odd-Double or the Even-Pinch alignments when utilizing this technique. The Forcing Unit (8-Man) applies our Gap principle by pinching off and then covering every offensive gap along the line of scrimmage.

An Odd-Double-Pinch call is an ideal alignment to pinch off the Tackle-Gap. On an Odd-Double-Pinch call the defensive corners pinch down inside three steps to the outside shoulder of the tight end. From this position they key the offensive play action, and then they execute their outside containment responsibilities. They become either the front side or the back side contain men with the offensive flow either towards them or away from them. The defensive ends and tackles pinch down into their inside gaps, to control these gaps. And, according to the offensive play action, they must pick up any offensive backs hitting into their respective areas.

The middle guard uses a Control technique. He keys the offensive quarterback and the flow of the backfield, and then he slides to the back side gap, away from flow, to cover this gap for a possible inside counter play.

The middle linebacker keys through the offensive guards to the quarterback and fullback. He will then key the offensive play action and check the Center Gap to the side of flow. He will fill this gap with action. If it is obvious that the play is going to the outside flank area, the middle linebacker will slide laterally along the line of scrimmage and then fill into the appropriate area (Diagram 5-1).

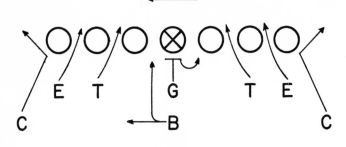

DIAGRAM 5-1
Odd-Double-Pinch

An Even-Pinch call is an ideal alignment for sealing off the inside Center Gaps. On an Even-Pinch call, the corners, ends, and tackles execute their inside Pinch techniques and assignments in the exact same manner as described for the Odd-Double-Pinch call. The inside linebackers key through the offensive tackles into the near back and the quarterback. On key, they call out the offensive play action. Their first responsibility is to fill the Guard-Gaps with action. If the play action is towards them but to the outside, they must slide laterally to the outside and then fill from an outside position. If play action is away, they become a middle linebacker checking for a possible inside counter play (Diagram 5-2).

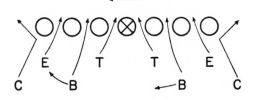

DIAGRAM 5-2
Even-Pinch

A pinch technique to the split end side is excellent from an Odd-Double call, as the Forcing Unit can pinch tough inside with an end in position to contain the outside and a corner in a walk-away position to double cover the split end. The techniques and coverages are identical as previously described for the Odd-Double-Pinch call. The only exception is that the defensive end to the split-end side becomes the back side contain man, with flow away from him (Diagram 5-3).

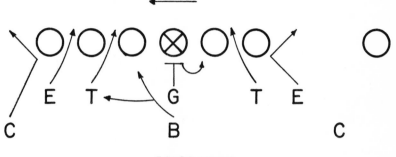

DIAGRAM 5-3
Odd-Double-Pinch

COORDINATED ATTACK TECHNIQUES

The purpose of the Attack technique is to get our Forcing Unit across the line of scrimmage so that they can destroy the offensive ball handling or tackle the ball carrier or quarterback for a loss of yardage. When attacking, we prefer to create an over-load effect at the anticipated point of attack. Thus, we can get more defensive men at the point of attack than there are offensive blockers.

The type of defensive alignment or Attack Plan that is called for will depend upon the offensive tendencies of our opponent, as described and illustrated from our scouting report. The following information will explain and illustrate how we organize our Attack Plans, with a description of the strengths of each plan.

We have had good success attacking the Tackle-Gap from an Odd-Double-Inside call. On an Odd-Double-Inside call, the defensive corners move to an Inside position to work as a unit with the defensive end and tackle. The middle guard and middle linebacker also work as a unit.

The defensive corners can either attack the Tackle-Gap or the Guard-Gap, depending upon the defensive call, with the defensive tackles automatically taking the opposite gap. The defensive ends align on the outside shoulder of the tight end and contain the outside flank area from this position. As this unit attacks on the snap of the ball, they must key the offensive play action, call it out, and then execute their assignments accordingly. With flow away, the defensive end becomes the outside contain man and the inside corner becomes an inside contain man, checking for a possible inside counter play.

The middle guard and the middle linebacker can attack both Center-Gaps on the snap of the ball through a predetermined call, or they can use their basic Double technique with the middle guard using a Control Charge and then checking the back side gap, with the middle linebacker keying and moving with the flow of the ball.

This Attack Plan is particularly tough versus an inside running game, because the middle linebacker is in an excellent position to support either Inside Corner from his middle-most position. Also, we get an over-load effect in the Tackle-Gap area with three defensive men versus two offensive blockers (Diagram 5-4).

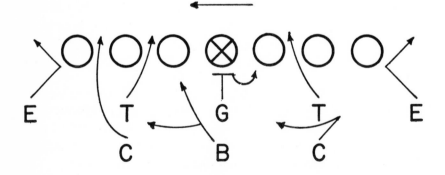

DIAGRAM 5-4
Odd-Double-Inside Tackle-Gap

When we need good outside support at the defensive corner area and we still want to attack the Tackle-Gap area, we use an Odd-Tackle-Gap call. This call gives us excellent support at both the Tackle-Gap and the corner areas at the same time. The corner to the strong side plays in his normal corner alignment. From this position, he must key the offensive play action, call it out, and then execute his specific assignment. Both inside linebackers slide into a position just inside their defensive tackles. From this position, they team up as a unit with the defensive tackles and ends to attack the Tackle-Gap to the side of flow. The back side linebacker away from the flow becomes a middle linebacker to check for a possible inside counter, and the defensive end to the strong side or the defensive corner (odd alignment) away from flow become the back side contain men to the outside flank areas.

The middle tackle (odd alignment) will use a Control Charge and then slide into the gap to the side of flow.

The entire Forcing Unit (8-Man) must key the offensive play action on the move, and then execute their specific assignments accordingly (Diagram 5-5).

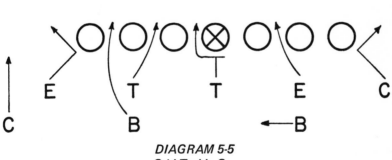

DIAGRAM 5-5
Odd-Tackle-Gap

Versus a split end formation, we prefer to use an Odd-Inside call. We can jump either our Power Corner or our Quick Corner men into an Inside attacking position. On an Odd-Power-Inside call, we would jump the Power Corner inside and drop off the Quick Corner to double cover the split end (Diagram 5-6).

On an Odd-Quick-Inside call, we would jump the Quick Corner inside and drop off the Power Corner to a corner alignment. This is an excellent adjustment towards a Flanker

Formation or to the wide side of the field (Diagram 5-7).

The basic attacking techniques and coverages and outside containment are identical to those previously described for the Odd-Inside-Double call.

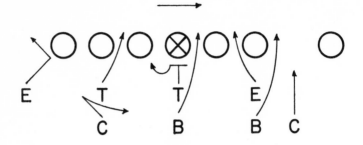

DIAGRAM 5-6
Odd-Power-Inside Tackle-Gap

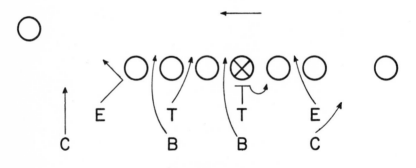

DIAGRAM 5-7
Odd-Quick-Inside Tackle-Gap

An Even-Tight alignment is an ideal alignment to attack the Guard-Gap, as we can get an over-load effect into this area. The inside linebackers stack behind the defensive ends and then work as a unit with the ends. On a Guard-Gap call the linebacker to the side of flow will attack the Guard-Gap, and the back side linebacker becomes a middle linebacker. The corners become the contain men both towards and away from flow.

The entire Forcing Unit attacks on the snap of the ball, with the ends taking the Tackle-Gaps and the tackles taking the

Center-Gaps. As they attack, they must key on the move and then execute their specific assignments accordingly (Diagram 5-8).

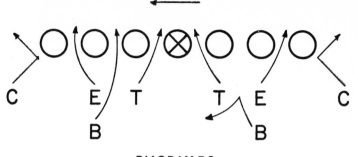

DIAGRAM 5-8
Even-Tight Guard-Gap

An alternate call would be an Even-Tight Tackle-Gap call with the linebacker to the side of flow taking the Tackle-Gap and the end taking the Guard-Gap.

If we want to attack the Guard-Gap or the Center-Gap and outside corner support at the same time, we would attack from an Even-Tight-Pro alignment. From this alignment, we would drop off the defensive corner to the strong side of the offensive formation or the wide side of the field. The middle linebacker would work with the defensive tackles and ends as a unit. On a Guard-Gap call the defensive tackles would attack the Center-Gaps and the defensive ends would attack the Tackle-Gaps. The middle linebacker would key the backfield flow and then attack the Guard-Gap to the side of flow. When we have definite tendencies on an opponent, we can predetermine or anticipate the side of flow and make a Guard-Gap call either to the right or left sides. In this case we would call an Even-Tight-Pro Guard-Gap-Left (Diagram 5-9).

As a change-up, we can attack both the Tackle-Gaps and the Guard-Gaps at the same time with four inside linebackers. This Attack Plan could be accomplished through an Even-Inside call.

The inside linebackers and the defensive tackles work as units, and the defensive ends and corners work as units. On the snap of the ball the linebackers and corners attack their called gaps to the side of flow, and the back side linebacker and corner

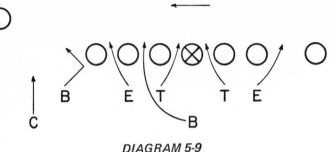

DIAGRAM 5-9
Even-Tight-Pro Guard-Gap-Left

become the back side contain men. It is possible to attack all eight men across the line of scrimmage at the same time without the employment of back side contain men, if so desired.

An example would be an Even-Inside Tackle-Guard-Gaps call (Diagram 5-10).

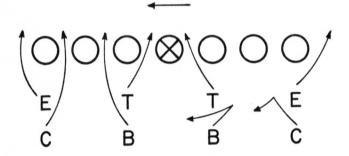

DIAGRAM 5-10
Even-Inside Tackle-Guard-Gap

We prefer to attack the Center-Gap from an Even-Stack or an Even-Split alignment. On an Even-Center-Gap call the linebackers team up with the defensive tackles. The linebacker to the side of flow would attack the Center-Gap, with the back side linebacker becoming a middle linebacker. Or, both men can attack both Center-Gaps at the same time on the snap of the ball. The ends attack the Tackle-Gaps and the corners become the outside contain men (Diagram 5-11).

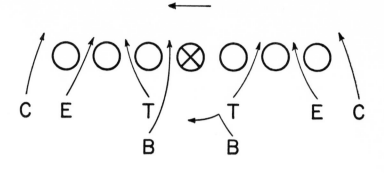

DIAGRAM 5-11
Even-Center-Gap

The assignments and coverages from an Even-Split Center-Gap call are identical as described for an Even-Center-Gap call. However, the linebackers have a slight advantage from this alignment as they can attack the Center-Gap from an inside gap position (Diagram 5-12).

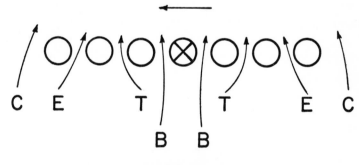

DIAGRAM 5-12
Even-Split Center-Gap

6

Coordinating the Slant
and Loop Techniques

COORDINATED SLANT TECHNIQUES

The purpose of the Slant technique is to get two men, the end and the corner, in an outside containing position. Versus a tight offensive line, we prefer to slant from an Even alignment, because we have both the end and the corner in excellent position on both sides of the line at the same time to execute this technique. We could either call a Slant Right or a Slant Left.

On a Slant Right call the defensive end and both of the defensive tackles away from the direction of the call would use a Slant technique into their inside gaps. The defensive corner away from the Slant call uses a Pinch technique moving to the outside shoulder of the tight end, and he becomes the contain man to his side with the flow either towards him or away from him.

The end to the side of the Slant call is aligned on the outside shoulder of the tight end, and he would use an outside control technique. It is his job to contain the outside with flow either towards him or away from him. The corner to the side of the Slant call moves into a defensive corner or a walk-away position, and from this position he prepares to cover the flat or help contain an outside running play.

The inside linebacker to the side of the Slant call aligns in a head-up position over the offensive tackle. With the flow towards him, he will fill tough into the Tackle-Gap. With flow away from him he will become a middle linebacker checking for an inside counter play. The linebacker away from the Slant call aligns in a stack position behind the defensive tackle. With action towards him, he fills tough into the Guard-Gap. With flow away from him he checks for an inside counter play Diagram (6-1).

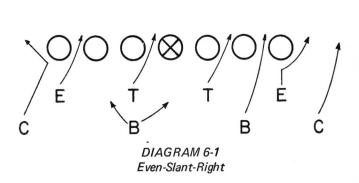

DIAGRAM 6-1
Even-Slant-Right

Many teams use the Slant technique quite successfully from and Odd alignment versus a tight line. This technique can be run effectively to the side of the end-corner combination. However, this defensive front alignment is overshifted and it is impossible for us (within our system of play) to get our end-corner combination to the weak side of this defensive front. For this reason, we prefer to use an Even alignment versus a tight formation (Diagram 6-2).

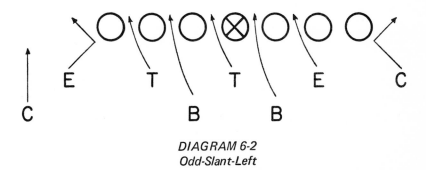

DIAGRAM 6-2
Odd-Slant-Left

Versus a split-end formation, we can slant effectively from either an Odd or an Even alignment. We can get our end-corner combination to either side at the same time and still fill every gap to the inside with the Forcing Unit.

The corner away from the Slant call must move up into a tight pinching position. From this position, he will use an inside Pinch technique into the outside shoulder of the tight end or the weak side tackle to the split-end side. He becomes the contain man to his side, with flow either towards him or away from him. The corner to the side of the Slant call plays in his normal corner position, as previously described.

The inside linebackers play head-up over the uncovered linemen as illustrated in Diagrams 6-3 and 6-4. They key in the same manner as previously described, and they fill tough into their inside gaps with flow towards them or they become a middle linebacker with flow away from them. The other interior linemen slant into their inside gaps and execute their responsibilities as previously described.

We prefer to slant to the split end in most instances, as this technique places our corner in the basic corner position to help double-cover the split end. However, we also like to slant to the tight end towards the wide side of the field or towards a Flanker formation (Diagrams 6-3 and 6-4).

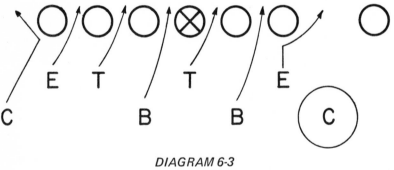

DIAGRAM 6-3
Odd-Slant-Right

We prefer to slant with two inside linebackers, as we can cover the inside Center-Gaps more effectively than with a single middle linebacker. This is true because we can cover the inside Center-Gap to the side of flow with an inside linebacker and still have a second inside linebacker in position to act as a middle

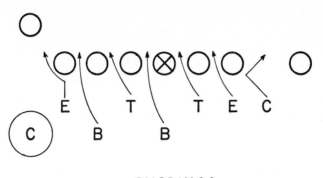

DIAGRAM 6-4
Even-Slant-Left

linebacker to check the back side Center-Gap for counter action. This is a definite weakness in trying to slant from a 53 corner defense (Diagram 6-5).

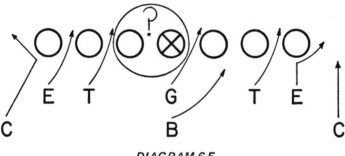

DIAGRAM 6-5
Odd-Double-Slant-Right

COORDINATED LOOP TECHNIQUES

The purpose of the Loop technique is to provide our Forcing Unit with a moving control type of defense. We use an Even alignment when looping versus a tight line.

The end and corner to the side of the loop call the play in the same manner as previously described for the Slant technique.

The corner, end, and both tackles away from the directional call loop down one man to their inside to a head-up position. The linebacker away from the directional call also slides over one man on the snap of the ball, and the linebacker to the side of the call stacks in behind his tackle to cover the area vacated by this looping tackle.

Through this looping technique, we follow our Man principle in covering every offensive blocker along the line of scrimmage. In reality, we are sliding into an Odd 52 Corner defense. We would use the Loop technique for the same reasons as described for the Slant technique, the only difference being the use of looping control technique as opposed to the slanting gap technique. There are specific game situations when one technique is better than the other, and these situations will be covered in detail in Chapters 15 and 16 (Diagram 6-6).

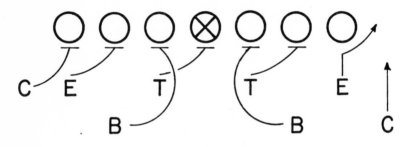

DIAGRAM 6-6
Even-Loop-Right

Versus a split-end formation, we like to Loop towards the split end from an Odd alignment and to the tight end or Flanker formation from an Even alignment. This is true because we position our defensive ends on the outside shoulder of the tight end and the weak side tackle. It is their assignment to cover these men, using our Man principle, and then contain the outside running plays with flow either towards them or away from them. Thus it is not necessary to loop our defensive tackles out in position to cover these outside offensive linemen (tight end and weak side tackle). Rather, the tackles loop in the direction of the call, with the inside linebackers looping in the opposite direction of the call to fill the areas vacated by the tackles. They merely exchange places. Through this looping technique our six interior defensive men can employ our Man principle to cover the six offensive blockers (Diagrams 6-7 and 6-8).

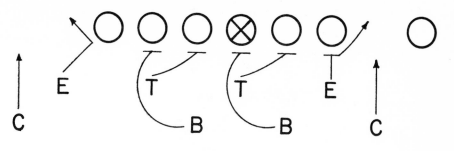

DIAGRAM 6-7
Odd-Loop-Right

Looping versus a split-end formation offers the defensive secondary many possibilities, because we can drop off both of our corners into a 5-Man secondary to enhance our pass defensive coverages.

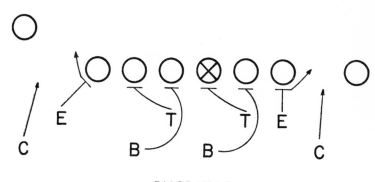

DIAGRAM 6-8
Even-Loop-Left

Versus a team that flip-flops, we would call the Loop technique in the direction of the formation. We would automatically align in an Even alignment, anticipating a possible tight formation, and then slide into an Odd alignment when looping towards the split end. The Forcing Unit merely calls out the name of the formation, such as split end left, and then they would execute their Loop technique towards the split end. This same approach would be used when looping towards a Flanker formation.

7

Coordinating Combination
Defensive Calls

HOW THE COMBINATION DEFENSE
SYSTEM IS ORGANIZED

Our defensive call system provides the flexibility to include the utilization of different types of defensive line techniques that can be used to each side of the defensive line at the same time. On a Combination call, the corner, end, tackle, and linebacker on each side of the defensive line work independently as a unit. For example, the defensive quarterback could call an Odd-Tackle-Gap-Left and a Control-Right. Through such a call as this one, the left defensive unit would attack the Tackle-Gap and the right defensive unit would control their right side (Diagram 7-1).

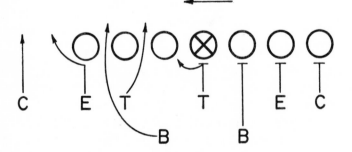

DIAGRAM 7-1
Odd-Tackle-Gap-Left Control-Right

On a Combination call the defensive quarterback always calls the defensive technique to be used to the left side first, and then he calls the technique to be used to the right side. Through the utilization of five basic techniques such as Pinch, Slant, Attack, Loop, and Control, in combination, it is possible to design 20 separate defensive calls that could be used with each defensive front alignment. We have 12 possible front alignments. Thus, it is possible to design over 240 different defensive calls. Of course, we have never used all of the 12 possible defensive front alignments during any one season, and we have not used all of the possible Combination calls during a specific season. To the contrary, we select only á few front alignments with a minimum number of Combination calls. However, with such fantastic built-in flexibility the defensive coach can design tailor-made defensive calls to counter the strengths of each offensive opponent. This is a big advantage as each offensive opponent, from week to week, usually gives a different look or has different personnel strengths or weaknesses, and we can change our defensive calls from week to week to meet the differences in offensive opponents.

We particularly like to Attack one side and either Control or Pinch the back side. We have found that some of our opponents, from specific formations, like to run direct plays to the strength of their formation and then use counter type plays, off this same backfield action, to the back side or weak side of their formation. If an opponent features effective outside counter type plays, we would use a Control technique to the back side or, if our opponent ran effective inside counter plays, we would use a Pinch technique to the back side. If our opponent had definite tendencies according to field position or down and yardage, we would mix up our back side calls, using either Pinch or Control according to these tendencies (Diagrams 7-1 and 7-2).

The defensive coach and the defensive quarterback must check out each combination call to be sure it is sound, as we must not leave a big hole in our defensive front alignment. In order for each call to be sound, the call must adhere to our Man-Gap principle in area coverage. Refer to Diagrams 7-3 to 7-22, which illustrate Odd alignment Combination calls versus a split-end formation. Diagrams 7-15 to 7-18 are shown from an Even alignment.

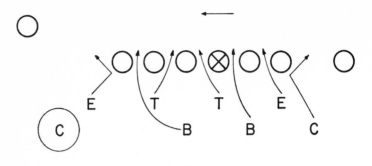

DIAGRAM 7-2
Odd-Tackle-Gap-Left Pinch-Right

This system may seem complicated because of the many possibilities. However, once the Forcing Unit has learned the defensive call system, as previously illustrated, and how to execute each defensive technique, they have learned the basic requirements for this system. The defensive coach can select a few of these defensive front alignments along with the defensive line techniques that he feels best meet the needs or physical capabilities of his personnel. The defensive coach could design an Even battery of defensive alignments, or just an Odd battery of defensive alignments. He may prefer to use just one Even alignment and one Odd alignment.

Again, we select from this multiple system of defenses a few variations that best meet the needs of our personnel and best suit the anticipated offensive formations and offensive play action of our opponents. We have never used this entire system at the high school level. However, this multiple system has the "built-in" flexibility to easily adapt or change from year to year to meet the needs of different defensive personnel or to adjust to new offensive trends without changing our basic system.

EXAMPLES AND ILLUSTRATIONS OF
COMBINATION DEFENSIVE CALLS

The use of descriptive terms has had a great deal to do with simplifying this combination call system, as each call on either side of the defensive line, by name, specifically tells each defensive unit exactly what to do, as illustrated in Diagrams 7-3 to 7-22.

It's possible, by manipulating the combination calls, to devise a brand new defense in preparation for the next opponent. And, as incredible as it may seem, no new learning is involved in this, as the five basic techniques always remain constant as they are applied to the various front alignments.

Another advantage of this system is that it makes it very difficult for opposing scouts to determine our defensive line patterns from week to week, as these patterns are constantly changing according to the offensive strengths and weaknesses of our opponents. As a result, our opponents can never be sure of what defenses we intend to utilize against them. This element of surprise gives the defense a big advantage.

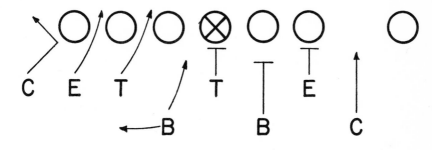

DIAGRAM 7-3
Pinch-Left
Control-Right

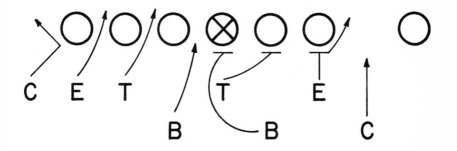

DIAGRAM 7-4
Pinch-Left
Loop-Right

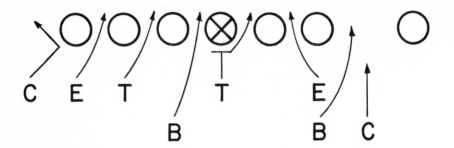

DIAGRAM 7-5
Pinch-Left
Tackle-Gap-Right

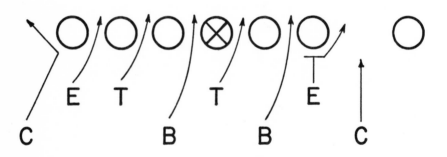

DIAGRAM 7-6
Slant-Right

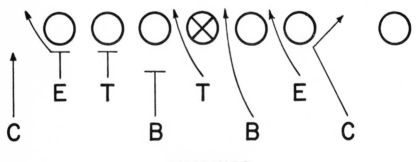

DIAGRAM 7-7
Control-Left
Pinch-Right

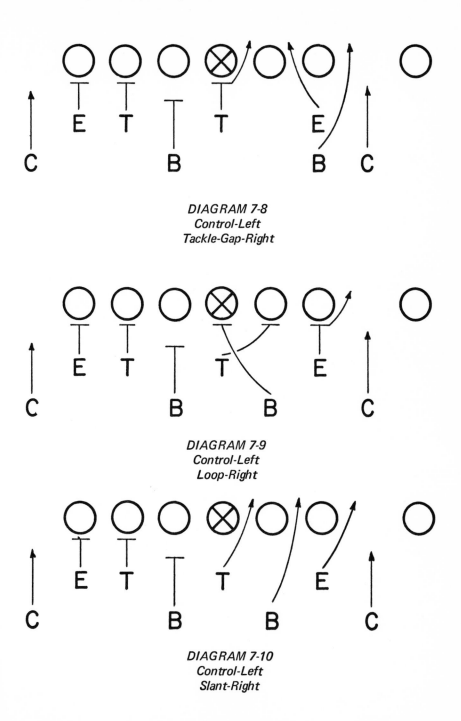

DIAGRAM 7-8
Control-Left
Tackle-Gap-Right

DIAGRAM 7-9
Control-Left
Loop-Right

DIAGRAM 7-10
Control-Left
Slant-Right

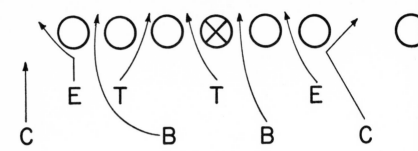

DIAGRAM 7-11
Tackle-Gap-Left
Pinch-Right

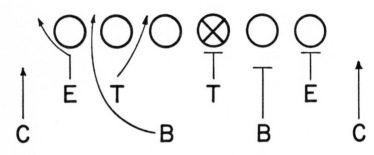

DIAGRAM 7-12
Tackle-Gap-Left
Control-Right

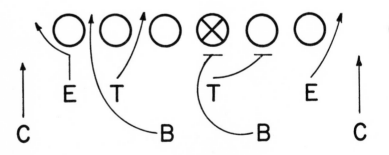

DIAGRAM 7-13
Tackle-Gap-Left
Loop-Right

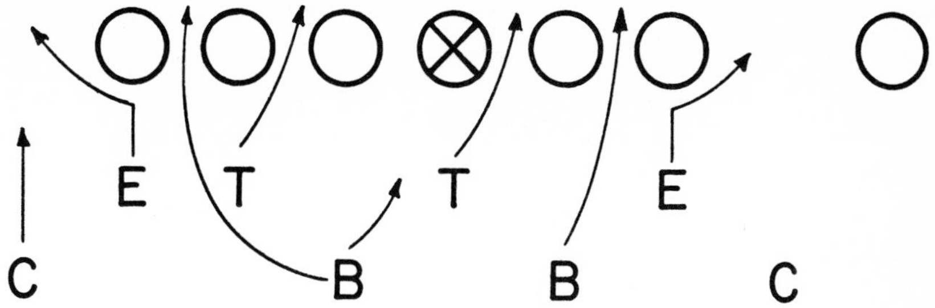

DIAGRAM 7-14
Tackle-Gap-Left
Slant-Right

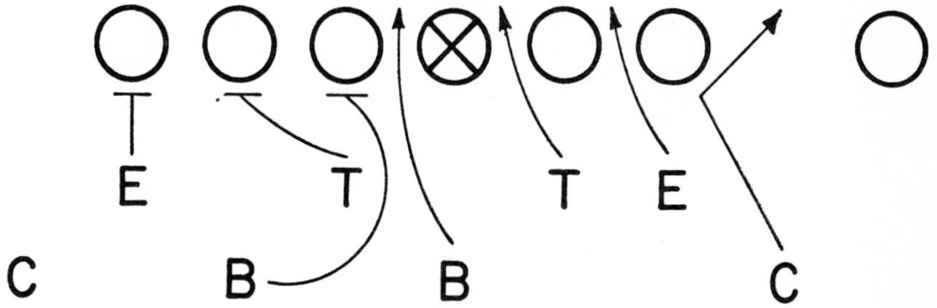

DIAGRAM 7-15
Loop-Left
Pinch-Right

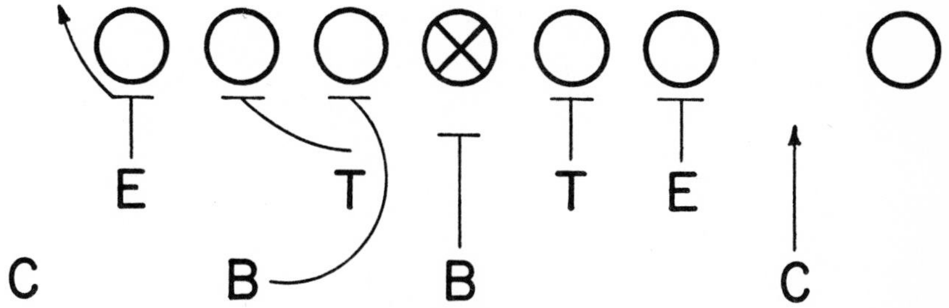

DIAGRAM 7-16
Loop-Left
Control-Right

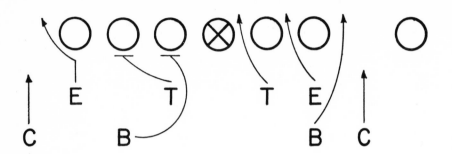

DIAGRAM 7-17
Loop-Left
Tackle-Gap-Right

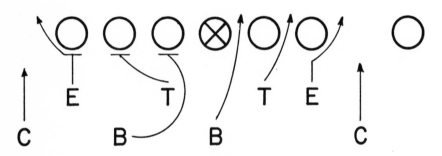

DIAGRAM 7-18
Loop-Left
Slant-Right

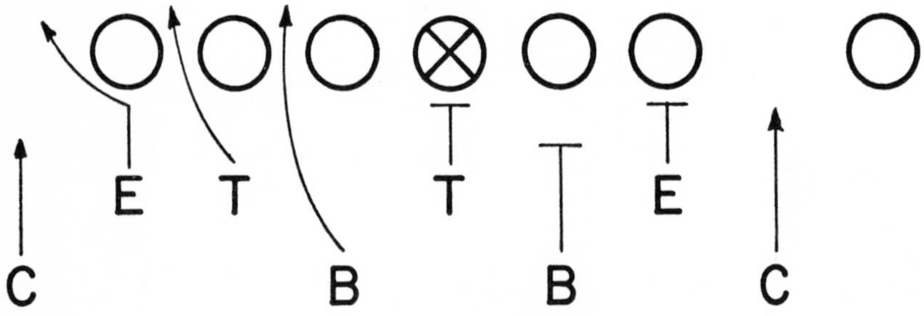

DIAGRAM 7-19
Slant-Left
Control-Right

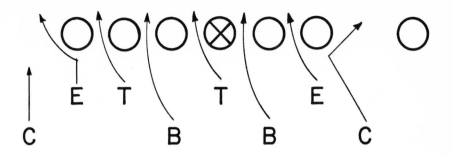

DIAGRAM 7-20
Slant-Left

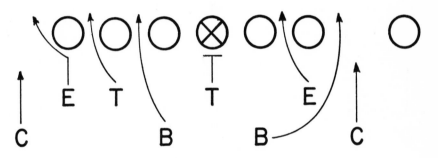

DIAGRAM 7-21
Slant-Left
Tackle-Gap-Right

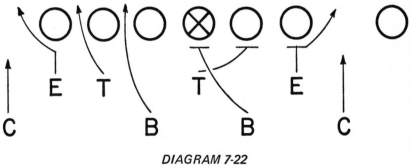

DIAGRAM 7-22
Slant-Left
Loop-Right

8

Coordinating the Forcing Unit
Versus Pass

COORDINATED CONTROL TECHNIQUES

Versus a Tight alignment, we employ the basic Even alignment on a passing down. In our opinion, this is the best pass defensive alignment in football versus a Tight formation.

This alignment places the defensive tackles in a head-up position over the offensive guards. From this position they execute a Control technique as they key through the quarterback to the fullback. We assign the left defensive tackle, because he is aligned to our opponent's right side, to key the near back (halfback or fullback) for a possible draw up the middle. The left tackle is assigned to key draw as most teams tend to be right-handed. If there is no draw, he should force the quarterback from an inside position. The right tackle puts on a hard rush from an inside position and attempts to throw the quarterback for a loss in yardage. If an opponent displays a tendency to draw to his left side, we can assign the right tackle to key draw.

As soon as the quarterback puts the ball up to throw, the tackles are instructed to get their hands up high to block the pass. If they cannot tackle the quarterback or block the pass and the quarterback is able to get the pass off, the tackles must turn and sprint back towards the ball. We want them in good position to block for the defensive back in case of an interception.

The defensive ends are aligned head-up over the tight ends. It is their first job to hold up the tight ends with a good forearm rip-up for at least two counts. From this position, they key through the near back to their side for a possible screen pass. Versus a tight formation the defensive corner is responsible for screen. Thus, the end is free to put on a good pass rush from an outside-in position playing the outside shoulder of the quarterback, keeping outside leverage on him at all times. As soon as the quarterback puts his hand up to pass, the ends should get their hands up high and try to block the pass. After the pass is thrown the ends must sprint back to the ball, getting into position to block in case of an interception. It should be noted, however, that if he keys screen, we want him to help contain this play by assisting the corner from an inside position.

Inside linebackers read the uncovered linemen to the quarterback and near back. If linemen show pass blocking and the quarterback drops back, they first check the near back for a possible draw for two counts and then move back to the inside hook zone. If the defensive ends hold up the tight ends for two counts, the inside backers will have time to key draw and assist the defensive tackles. If not, linebackers will have to leave sooner.

Linebackers must stagger their outside foot slightly back so that they can open up to the outside quickly from their inside position. As they open up on the move, they immediately key the tight end on a man-to-man basis and prepare to cover him on any type of short pass to the inside. Our hook zone area encompasses an area extending from the outside shoulder of the tight end to the offensive center in width, to a depth of ten yards (Diagram 8-1). We do not want our linebacker to sprint back to the hook zone as such, as we have found that a smart tight end will run a short look-in pass in front of him or run a curl-in pattern around him to the inside. By opening up into a parallel position and staying to the inside of the receiver at all times, he is in an excellent position to see the quarterback and play the tight end and the ball at the same time. From this inside position, he will cover the tight end in the same manner as described for the corner man when covering a split end moving into the inside seam area or streak zone.

If the tight end runs a deep route, the linebacker should immediately move out and check the flat area for a possible screen or swing pass. If the ball is passed deep, they must sprint back to the ball to cushion underneath or to be in position to block in case of an interception.

The linebacker is in good position to key screen, as the uncovered tackle to his side usually uses a check block and then pulls out to form a wall for the ball carrier. If the linebacker detects this move, he will give a screen call and then help contain this play from an inside position.

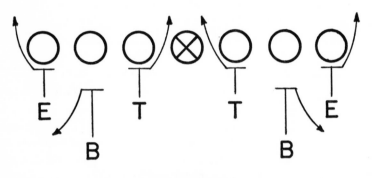

DIAGRAM 8-1
Even-Control

Versus a Split-End formation, we prefer an Odd alignment. The Odd alignment places the Quick Backer in a better position to cover the halfback in the flat or swing areas, and it places the middle tackle in an excellent position to key draw.

To the side of the split end, the Quick Backer must align in a head-up position over the halfback. From this position, he will key him for draw, screen, swing, or flat pass. He must cover the halfback man-to-man on any short pass outside. We do not feel that there is any danger of a hook or quick pass inside to the split end side because of the lack of a tight end to this side. Since the Quick Backer has the halfback man-to-man on short patterns, he can easily pick him up if he runs a short pass into this area (Diagram 8-2).

The Power Backer executes his basic keys and then covers his hook area. The defensive end to the split end side does not have to hold up the weak side offensive tackle, as he is not an eligible pass receiver. Thus he can put an immediate pass rush on the quarterback. The defensive end and tackle to the tight end side will also strive to put a tough pass rush on the quarterback (Diagram 8-2).

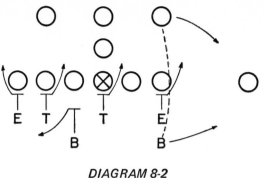

DIAGRAM 8-2
Odd-Control

We also use an Odd alignment versus a Flanker-Split-End or a Pro formation. However, we are forced to make an adjustment with our defensive end to the Flanker side. Here the defensive end must key the near back for a screen or flat pass. This is true because the corner to this side must drop off to cover the seam area (streak zone) between the tight end and the flanker. Since the defensive end holds up the tight end for two counts, the timing is just about right for keying the screen pass, as most backs will delay about two counts faking a pass block before running the screen pattern (Diagram 8-3). The rest of our Forcing Unit's responsibilities remain the same.

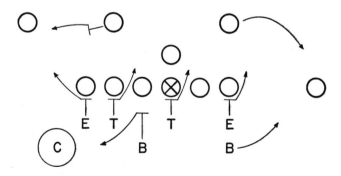

DIAGRAM 8-3
Odd-Control vs. Flanker

COORDINATED ATTACK
TECHNIQUES

We believe that there are times when the defense must have a plan for attacking the quarterback. This is particularly true when the defensive secondary cannot stop an outstanding passer via our Control Pass Defense, which features zone pass coverage.

Most of our opponents operate from a split-end formation, and we especially like to attack this split-end side. This is true because of the lack of blockers to this side of the formation and the fact that many teams prefer to release the halfback on pass patterns to the split-end side. When we see this tendency, we immediately attack the quarterback.

The Forcing Unit aligns in an Even alignment with both of the inside linebackers stacked behind the defensive tackles. From this alignment they attack either the Center or Guard gaps, or we can have one backer attack the Center-Gap with the other backer attacking the Guard-Gap. We like to mix up the attack combinations so that the offensive blockers never know for sure which gaps they will attack.

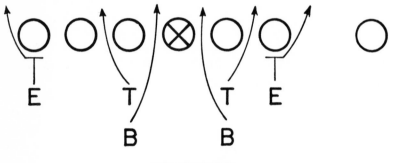

DIAGRAM 8-4
Even-Center Gaps

The defensive tackles take the opposite gap from the gap that is called for the linebackers, as they work as a unit with the inside linebackers. The defensive ends use a Control charge and then they rush the passer from an outside-in position. They must contain the quarterback and not let him scramble to the outside. We use a 5-deep man-to-man pass defense in the secondary so that the defensive end to the tight end side does not have to cover the near back for a screen or flat pass, and both of our linebackers are free to attack as they are free from their pass coverage duties (Diagram 8-4).

PART III

HOW TO COORDINATE THE 53 MULTIPLE CONTAINING UNIT

9

Coaching the Containing Unit Versus Run

The Containing Unit includes two corners (power and quick), two halfbacks, and a safety. These men coordinate as a unit to key and then contain the outside running game. They specifically key and then contain such plays as the sweep, quick toss, belly or split-T option, and the quarterback roll out or sprint out to the side of flow. To the back side away from flow, they are responsible to key and then contain an outside reverse or a bootleg run.

The following information will provide a general description as to how the Containing Unit executes their basic outside rotation and containment techniques. Specific keys and team coverages versus the above-mentioned outside running plays will be covered in detail in Chapters 15 and 16.

COACHING 3-ROTATE TECHNIQUES

The purpose of the 3-Rotate secondary technique is to provide quick outside containment to support the Forcing Unit that is either attacking or pinching to the inside. Thus the 3-Rotate technique is used in conjunction with our Pinching and Attacking defenses.

The 3-Rotate is also used versus Tight offensive formations. This is true because the defensive halfbacks must rotate up from their tight alignment to help contain the outside running game.

Versus a split formation our defensive halfbacks must move out to cover the wide receiver for pass. Therefore, in our opinion, they are not in good position to support the run, as they must be pass conscious first.

The defensive Containing Unit executes the 3-Rotate technique versus run as follows. To the side of flow, the corner, from a tight pinching or attacking position, must force the run and contain the outside; the halfback slides laterally three steps while keying the tight end. If the tight end is still blocking at the end of the halfback's third step, the halfback keys run and then rotates up fast to the outside to support the corner on outside containment. The safety rotates back into the deep one third or Out zone vacated by the safety, and the back side corner rotates back to the back side deep one third or Out zone. This rotation places our secondary in a 3-deep alignment (Diagram 9-1). The basic techniques used in rotation such as body position, shedding, and tackling are covered in detail in Chapter 14.

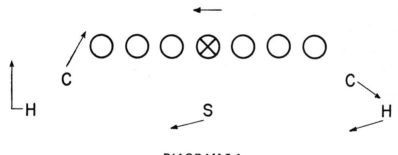

DIAGRAM 9-1
(3-Rotate Technique)

COACHING 4-ROTATE TECHNIQUES

The purpose of the 4-Rotate technique versus run is to get both the end and the corner men to the outside to contain and still maintain a 4-deep secondary at the same time. This rotation technique is used in conjunction with the Control, Slant, and Loop outside techniques.

This outside coverage enables the end to contain the outside, which frees the corner to either cover the flat, drop off to double-cover a split receiver, or to pick up the pitch man on an outside quarterback keep or pitch play. The 4-Rotate provides excellent coverage versus split end or flanker formations and to the wide side of the field. Also, this rotation provides excellent back side coverage versus reverse action plays, as illustrated in Chapters 10 and 17.

The defensive secondary executes the 4-Rotate technique as follows. To the side of the flow, the defensive end contains the outside, the corner supports run to the outside from a corner alignment, the halfback supports the corner on run from an inside position, and the safety rotates to the deep Out zone versus a tight formation and to the deep Streak zone versus a split formation. The back side halfback rotates to the deep Center zone versus a tight formation, and the back side corner rotates to the deep Out zone versus a tight formation and to the deep Center zone versus a split formation to the back side. This rotation places the secondary in a 4-deep alignment (Diagrams 9-2 and 9-3).

Specific 4-Rotate coverages versus favorite outside running plays are covered in detail in Chapters 15 and 16.

As the Containing Unit executes the 4-Rotate technique, they must key through the first receiver to their inside into the near back and quarterback. And, upon recognition of the specific offensive play action, they must call out this play action and then execute their assignments and coverages accordingly.

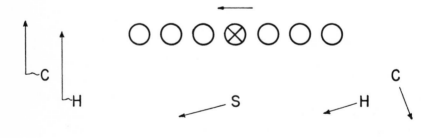

DIAGRAM 9-2
(4-Rotate vs. Tight Formation)

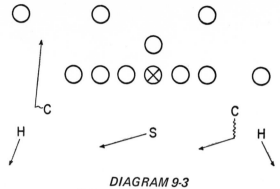

DIAGRAM 9-3
(4-Rotate vs. Pro Formation)

COACHING SAFETY BLITZ
TECHNIQUES

The purpose of the Safety Blitz technique is to place the defensive safety in a good position, versus a split formation, to support an attacking or pinching corner in outside containment.

Since the defensive halfbacks are removed to an outside position to cover a split receiver, they cannot rotate up as fast to support a tight corner as they could from a 3-Rotate versus a tight formation. To compensate for this problem, the safety man slides into a halfback alignment (or typical 4-deep alignment) to the side of the tight corner and the split receiver. From this position the safety can support the corner man outside in a hurry. He will take three lateral steps to the outside as he reads the tight end or the halfback (split end side) and then move up if this tight receiver is blocking and he keys run. His movement and containing technique is identical to the halfback on a 3-Rotate.

If the back side of the offensive formation away from the Flanker or Split End is tight, the halfback to this side will remain in his normal halfback alignment with the corner aligned in his basic corner alignment. This places our secondary in a 3-deep alignment (Diagram 9-4).

With flow of the ball towards the split receiver, the corner would force to the outside, with the safety supporting him. The back side halfback to the tight side rotates to the deep Center zone, with the back side corner rotating back to his deep Out zone. Refer to Diagrams 9-4 and 9-5 for our Safety Blitz containment technique versus a Flanker and a Split End formation. With the flow to the tight side of the offensive formation, we would use a 4-Rotate to this tight side. (Again, refer to Diagrams 9-4 and 9-5).

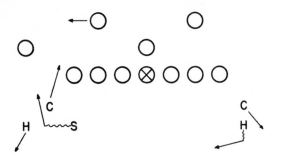

DIAGRAM 9-4
Safety Blitz to Flanker

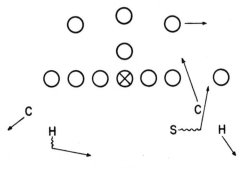

DIAGRAM 9-5
Safety Blitz to Split End

Versus a Pro formation, the corner away from the Safety Blitz call would rotate back into a basic 4-deep alignment. This alignment would place him directly over the tight receiver to his side, either the tight end or halfback, and he would key this man on a man-to-man basis. To the split end side, if the offensive halfback leaves with the flow towards the flanker, the corner would rotate back over the deep Center zone. With flow to the split end, the corner would support the outside run, with the safety rotating back over the Center zone. However, the safety must key the tight end and keep him to his inside as he rotates straight back initially, and then over to the Center zone. This is true because he has the tight end man-to-man and in case of a play action pass he would have to be in position to cover him.

(See Diagrams 9-6 and 9-7 for a Safety Blitz call versus a Pro formation towards either the Flanker or the Split End sides.)

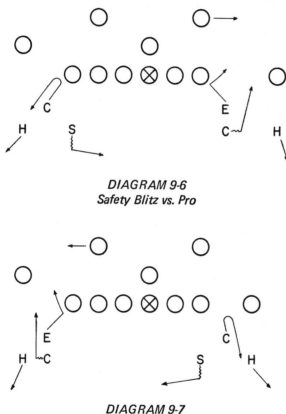

DIAGRAM 9-6
Safety Blitz vs. Pro

DIAGRAM 9-7
Safety Blitz vs. Pro

COACHING EAGLE TECHNIQUES

The purpose of the Eagle containment technique is to provide a change-up in outside containment versus split formations and still maintain a 5-deep secondary to execute the 4-Rotate technique. The difference in this technique from the basic 4-Rotate is that the linebacker contains the outside, with the end attacking his inside gap. They merely exchange assignments.

Versus a Flanker formation, we would use an Even-Eagle alignment. This alignment places our linebacker in an ideal position to contain the outside, as he slides to a position just slightly to the inside shoulder of the defensive end. From this position the linebacker and end work as a unit. With flow to them, the end would attack the inside gap, with the linebacker moving quickly to his outside and across the line of scrimmage. From this position he would get into a proper hitting position and prepare to contain the outside. The secondary would use a 4-Rotate (Diagram 9-8).

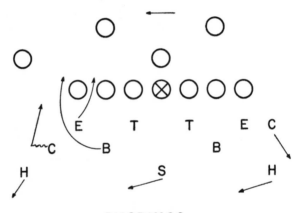

DIAGRAM 9-8
Eagle Containment vs. Flanker

To the split end side we would use an Odd alignment, as this alignment places our inside linebacker in an Eagle alignment. The end and linebacker would use the Eagle technique with the secondary in a 4-Rotate (Diagram 9-9).

If we wanted to attack our corner across the line of scrimmage and at the same time maintain our deep middle safety, we would use an Eagle Flat coverage technique. Through this coverage, on key our inside Eagle linebacker would cover the flat with the corner containing the outside. The rest of the secondary would use a 4-Rotate technique (Diagram 9-10).

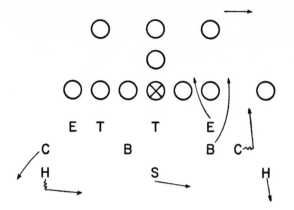

DIAGRAM 9-9
Eagle Containment vs. Split End

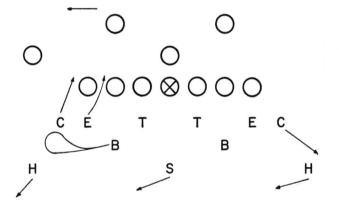

DIAGRAM 9-10
Eagle Flat Technique

It is also possible to use Eagle containment versus a tight formation. We would use an Even alignment so that both linebackers would be in an Eagle position to both sides of the line at the same time. We would use this technique in conjunction with an attacking corner and a 3-Rotate in the secondary (Diagram 9-11).

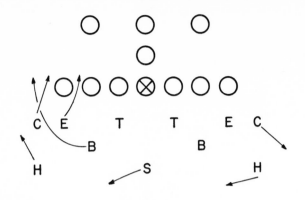

DIAGRAM 9-11
Eagle vs. Tight Formation

COACHING SAFETY ATTACK
TECHNIQUES

It is possible to attack the safety from either an Odd or an Even alignment. Versus a tight offensive formation, we prefer to attack the safety into the Tackle-Gap from an Odd alignment. This gives us an over-load effect into this running area, and at the same time provides our defense with excellent inside and outside support versus the run (Diagram 9-12).

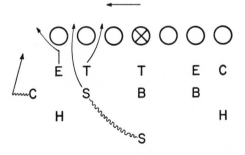

DIAGRAM 9-12
Odd-Safety-Tackle-Gap-Left

Versus a tight formation, we prefer to attack either the Guard or Center gaps from an Even alignment. The safety would jump into a middle linebacker position and then attack the called gap. (See Diagram 9-13 which illustrates an Even-Safety-Guard-Gap-Left call.)

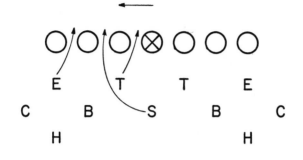

DIAGRAM 9-13
Even-Safety-Guard-Gap-Left

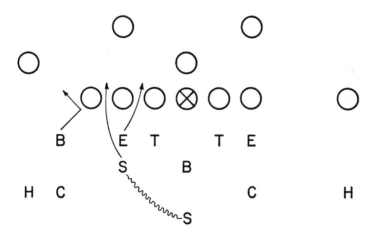

DIAGRAM 9-14
Even-Tight-Pro-Safety-Tackle-Gap

Versus tight offensive formations our secondary aligns in a 2-deep alignment with our halfbacks head-up over the tight ends. The corners align in either an attacking position on the line of scrimmage or in their basic corner alignment, depending upon the defensive call. From this secondary alignment we play man-to-man coverage, with the halfbacks taking the tight ends and the corners taking the halfbacks. The interior linemen and the safety are instructed to tackle the fullback if he hits into their area of coverage so that he cannot sneak through the line as a fifth receiver on a play-action pass.

Versus a Split-End or a Pro formation, we prefer to attack the safety from an Even-Tight-Pro alignment. This defensive alignment covers the offensive linemen man for man. Thus, we can attack the safety into any of the inside gaps to get an over-load effect completely down the line of scrimmage. The secondary goes into a 4-deep alignment and uses man-to-man secondary coverage (Diagram 9-14).

10

Coaching the Containing Unit Versus Roll-Out and Play-Action Passes

Our basic rotation and coverages for Roll-Out and Play-Action passes are identical, so these coverages are described under the same heading. The following information will explain how we cover this offensive play-action from our various secondary coverages.

We believe that it is very important to give defensive men specific assignments when covering a Roll-Out run or pass (we consider a Sprint-Out in the same category as the Roll-Out). In our opinion, one of the worst things a defensive coach can do to a secondary man is to place him in a situation where he has to make a choice whether to come up and contain or drop off and cover the flat. In this situation, a smart quarterback will take advantage of a confused secondary man, force him to make an error in judgment, and successfully run the proper option accordingly.

COORDINATED 3-ROTATE COVERAGES

As previously indicated, we prefer to use a 3-Rotate versus a tight offensive formation. Any time the quarterback either rolls out or sprints out with the football without faking the ball to an offensive back, we key Roll-Out all the way. The Containing Unit keys through the tight end or wing back to the near back and quarterback. On a 3-Rotate, on Roll-Out key, the corner will contain the quarterback. He must not let him turn the corner and he should try to tackle him behind the line of scrimmage. The halfback will slide laterally three steps keying the tight receiver and, as he sees the quarterback roll out with the tight receiver releasing, he will level off, yell "Roll-Out," and then cover the Flat. The safety and the back side halfback and corner men, away from Roll-Out, will rotate to cover the three deep zones to the side of flow (Diagram 10-1).

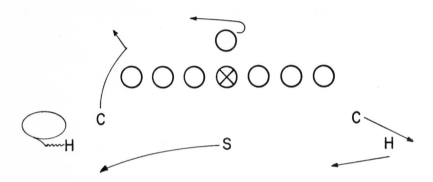

DIAGRAM 10-1
3-Rotate vs. Roll-Out

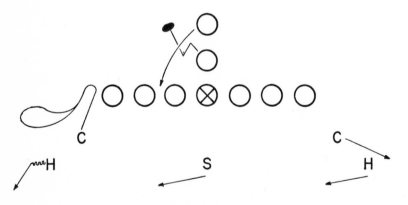

DIAGRAM 10-2
3-Rotate vs. Play-Action Pass

We use the same basic 3-Rotate coverage versus Play-Action passes. The corner and halfback to the side of flow will key as previously described and, if the tight receivers are releasing, even though the play looks like a run, they will yell "Pass" and move back into their pass zones. As soon as the Corner keys Play-Action pass, he will drop off into his Flat zone and play pass, as he does not have to contain the quarterback in this situation. If the defensive halfback keys Play-Action pass at the end of his third step, he will level off and drop back into his deep Out zone. The rest of the secondary rotates and we end up in a 4-Rotate or a 4-deep (Diagram 10-2).

As previously indicated, we use our Attacking and Pinching defenses in conjunction with the 3-Rotate to the side of tight end or wing back. We particularly like to use our Slanting defense, as we pinch our end and corner inside to the tight side of the formation, with our end to the side of the Slant call in an outside control position. This also places our corner man to the side of the Slant call in his basic corner alignment. From this corner alignment, he can easily rotate back to cover the deep Out zone away from the side of flow (Diagram 10-1). If our opponent rolls out to the side of the Slant call, the end would contain the quarterback, the corner would cover the Flat, and the deep secondary would cover their deep zones. Thus, we get a 3-Rotate to the Pinching side and a 4-Rotate to the Slanting side.

Versus an opponent that executes Roll-Out or Play-Action passes well, we would not want to get our back side corner into a tight alignment any more than necessary. However, if the back side corner is aligned in a tight or inside position, the halfbacks and safety will have to key on a man-to-man basis. To the side of flow, the safety will key the tight end as he rotates. If the tight end runs a Post pattern into the deep Center zone, the safety will have to cover him unless he gets a release call from the back side halfback. To the side of flow, the halfback must key the near back man-to-man and cover him. If he gets a release call from the safety, he will know that the safety is in position to cover the deep Out zone and that he can level off and cover his Flat versus Roll-Out. The back side halfback away from flow must cover the tight end man-to-man, and he will stay with this man unless he gets a release call from the back side corner. The back side corner keys the near back man-to-man. If the near back leaves with no bootleg, he will rotate back to the deep out zone. If he is in position to cover the tight end, he is free to release the halfback for rotation into the Center zone.

When using an Inside call the back side corner is not in

position to rotate back, so the halfback will have to cover the tight end man-to-man all the way (Diagrams 10-3 and 10-4). Play-action passes are covered in the same manner.

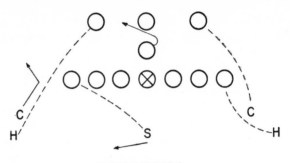

DIAGRAM 10-3
Tight Corners vs. Roll-Out

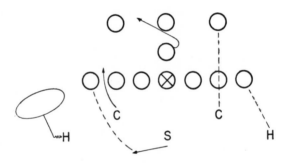

DIAGRAM 10-4
Inside Corners vs. Roll-Out

COORDINATED 4-ROTATE COVERAGES

We prefer to use a 4-Rotate versus split-end and flanker formations, because this rotation places our end in position to contain the quarterback with the corner in position to cover the Flat. This coverage also frees the halfback to cover the split receiver. However, we also like to use a 4-Rotate versus a Tight offensive formation that likes to flood a zone with three receivers. This coverage is shown in Chapter 17.

On a 4-Rotate versus split formations, we cover the Roll-Out and Play-Action passes, on key, in the same manner, the only difference being that they yell "Roll-Out" on Roll-Out action and "Pass" on Play-Action pass key. To the side of flow, the Containing Unit rotates into a 4-deep, as previously described (Diagrams 10-5 and 10-6).

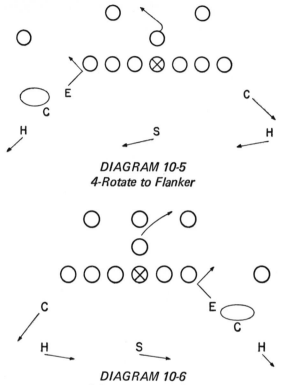

DIAGRAM 10-5
4-Rotate to Flanker

DIAGRAM 10-6
4-Rotate to Split End

COORDINATED SAFETY BLITZ AND EAGLE COVERAGES

We would cover roll-out or play-action passes from the Safety Blitz secondary alignment as follows. Versus a Pro formation with flow to the Flanker, the safety will key the tight end taking his three lateral steps to the outside. If the end releases, he will cover him man-to-man on pass. The back side corner to the split end side will key the halfback; if he moves with the flow on Roll-Out key, the corner will rotate over the Center zone and pick up the tight end over the middle to support the safety man. In this situation, he would give the safety a release call and then take the tight end. The outside halfbacks cover their split receivers man-to-man.

We use Eagle Flat coverage versus Roll-Out to the side of the Pinching or Attacking corner. To the Flanker side we would align in an Even alignment with the corner containing the quarterback and the linebacker covering the flat (Diagram 10-7).

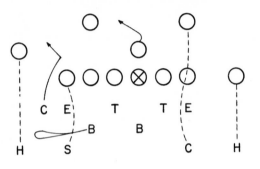

DIAGRAM 10-7
Safety Blitz and Eagle Flat Coverages

If the Safety Blitz call is towards the Flanker and the Roll-Out is run to the split end side, the end will contain the quarterback and the corner will take the halfback man-to-man. The safety and back side corner must cover man-to-man on the tight end near back away from flow to the Flanker side (Diagram 10-8).

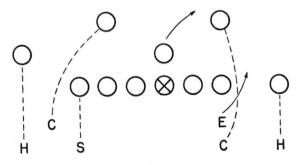

DIAGRAM 10-8
Roll-Out Coverage Away from Safety Blitz

With a Safety Blitz call to the split end side, the corner would contain the quarterback and the safety would cover the halfback man-to-man. In this coverage, the Power Corner would rotate back to a 4-deep alignment and cover the tight end man-to-man (Diagram 10-9).

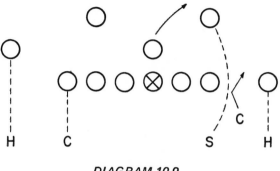

DIAGRAM 10-9
Safety Blitz vs. Roll-Out

Versus Play-Action passes, the inside linebacker will be held inside by a faking back. Thus we cannot use our Eagle Flat coverage to the Flanker side effectively. However, as soon as the corner recognizes the Play-Action pass he will drop back to cover the Flat to his side, keying the near back to his side. The rest of the secondary would cover man-to-man as described for Roll-Out coverage.

If we want to keep the safety in his deep Center zone and get a change-up in containment, we can use an Eagle containment

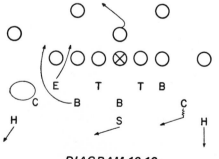

DIAGRAM 10-10
Eagle Containment to Flanker

technique. This technique is identical to the 4-Rotate coverage, with the end and linebacker exchanging assignments. The end either pinches or attacks the inside gap, with the linebacker containing the outside from an Eagle linebacker position. The rest of the secondary executes the basic 4-Rotate coverage (Diagrams 10-10 and 10-11).

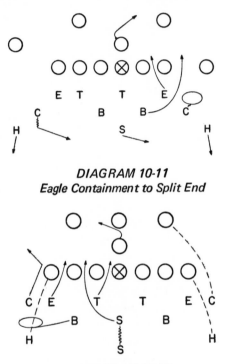

DIAGRAM 10-11
Eagle Containment to Split End

DIAGRAM 10-12
Eagle Flat Safety-Guard-Gap

COORDINATED SAFETY ATTACK
COVERAGES

If the safety is aligned in an inside attacking position versus a tight offensive formation, the halfbacks cover the tight ends man-to-man and the corners cover the near back to their side man-to-man. We would use either Eagle flat or Eagle containment outside coverages in conjunction with a 2-deep corner secondary

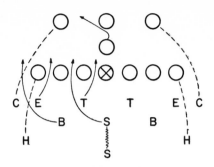

DIAGRAM 10-13
Eagle Contain Safety-Guard-Gap

alignment. See Diagrams 10-12 and 10-13. We would use Eagle flat coverage versus a Roll-Out pass (as shown in Diagram 10-12).

Versus a Play-Action pass, we instruct the safety and the interior linemen and linebackers to tackle any backs faking through the line, as some teams try to sneak a fifth back deep on a Post pattern in the Center zone.

Versus a Pro offensive formation, we use the same man-to-man coverage with our halfbacks and corners from a 4-deep secondary.

COORDINATED SECONDARY COVERAGES
OF REVERSE ACTION PASSES

We instruct the back side contain man to be alert for a possible Bootleg pass on every down. As soon as the near back leaves with the flow of the backfield, the contain man immediately keys the quarterback for a possible Bootleg. If the corner is in a tight alignment, he must key and then contain the quarterback on Bootleg. As previously indicated, with the corner in a tight alignment the secondary will have to key man-to-man. The secondary will start their initial flow with the flow of the backfield and then revert back into their original zones on Bootleg key. They must yell "Bootleg" and then cover their zones accordingly (Diagram 10-14).

If the secondary is positioned in our basic corner alignment, the end will contain the outside. Again, the secondary will start their flow and then revert back on Bootleg key. However, we get

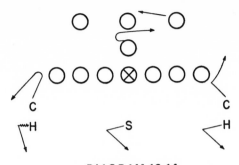

DIAGRAM 10-14
Corner Containment of Bootleg

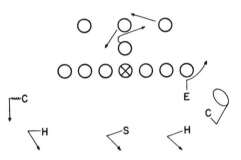

DIAGRAM 10-15
End Containment of Bootleg

better back side coverage with a back side corner and halfback in a 4-Rotate alignment (Diagram 10-15).

We key for a possible short Throw-Back pass on every Roll-Out play. If the quarterback flows one way but the near back runs a swing pattern opposite, the contain man immediately keys Throw-Back. It is the contain man's job, either the corner or end, to cover the short Throw-Back pass (Diagram 10-16).

Versus an opponent that throws a Bootleg or Throw-Back pass well from a split formation, we will definitely be in a 4-Rotate to the back side. This places the end in position to cover the short Throw-Back, the corner rotates back into the seam area between the split receiver and the tight receiver to cover this zone, and the back side halfback covers the deep Out zone. We believe that this secondary adjustment provides our secondary with excellent back side coverage versus the pass (Diagram 10-17).

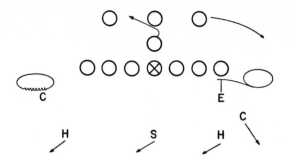

DIAGRAM 10-16
Roll-Out Throw-Back Coverage

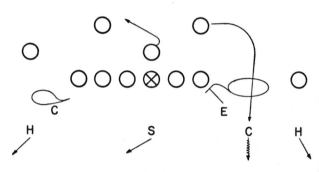

DIAGRAM 10-17
4-Rotate vs. Throw-Back Pass

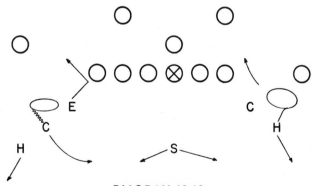

DIAGRAM 10-18
Hash Mark Coverage vs. Roll-Out

COORDINATED PASS COVERAGES
ACCORDING TO HASH MARK

Versus the Roll-Out and Play-Action passes, we use a 3-Rotate to the short side of the field and a 4-Rotate to the wide side of the field. To the short side of the field, we move the corner up to the line of scrimmage in a containing position, the halfback moves into an inside corner position on the split receiver (using the sideline as an extra man), and the safety man aligns in his basic Center zone. With flow to the short side the corner contains, the halfback covers the Flat, and the safety rotates to the deep Out zone. We have found that the safety can easily rotate to cover the Out zone to the short side of the field, as this zone represents one third of the field (Diagram 10-18).

11

Coaching the Containing Unit
Versus Drop-Back Pass

COACHING ZONE PASS DEFENSIVE
COVERAGES

Versus a tight offensive formation, we use a basic 3-deep zone pass defense with our halfbacks covering their deep one third or Out zones and the safety covering his middle one third or Center zone. The corners cover their Flat zones.

Anytime the quarterback drops straight back to pass, we automatically key Drop-Back pass, Screen, and Draw plays. On this key every man in the Containing Unit is instructed to yell "Pass" loud and clear.

On a passing down we automatically go into an Even alignment, with our corners dropped off into their basic corner alignment. From this alignment, they will open-up with the outside foot as they key through the tight end to the near back and quarterback. As the tight end releases, corners will start to angle back, getting depth into their Flat zones. This zone is ten yards deep and extends to the sideline. However, corners do not want to get too deep too fast. They must maintain a close enough relationship with the receiver to make an interception or to slap the ball down. They must execute all of the pass techniques described in Chapter 14.

Corners also key through the near back to their side for a possible Screen pass. With good vision and through much drilling, corners will see the Screen develop all the way and then get into position to stop it.

Halfbacks open-up to the outside and key in the same manner as described for the corners. As soon as the tight end releases they will angle back into their deep Out zone. Again, halfbacks must be careful not to get too deep or wide too fast. We want them to get depth, but be in position to properly play the receiver and the football as described for the corners. We want them to "jump" onto the receivers and play tough man-to-man coverage within their respective zones. Halfbacks must execute the pass defense techniques described in Chapter 14.

The safety must cover the deep Center zone. He will key through the guards to the quarterback and fullback. With the guards showing pass blocking and the quarterback dropping straight back, he automatically keys Pass. He is also in excellent position to see and key the Draw play, and he must yell "Draw" loud and clear if he detects this play. He is the last resort man, so he should strive to stay deeper than the football at all times so that he can make that desperation tackle of a break-away receiver if necessary. Also, he must execute the pass defense techniques that are described in Chapter 14 (Diagram 11-1).

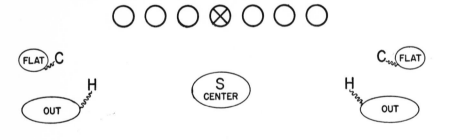

DIAGRAM 11-1
Even Zone Pass Defense

Versus one split receiver, such as a split end or flanker, we believe that we need a fourth defensive back to cover an additional zone created by this offensive formation. This additional zone is located in the seam area between the split receiver and the first tight receiver to his inside, which is the tight end (flanker side) and halfback (split end side). We refer to these zones as the Streak zones (Diagrams 11-2 and 11-3).

To compensate, we move the defensive corner into this Streak zone, which gives us a 4-deep secondary.

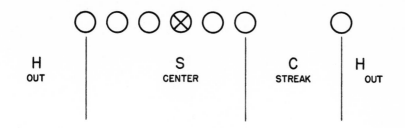

DIAGRAM 11-2
Streak Zone Split End Side

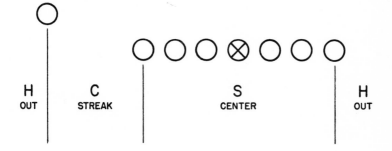

DIAGRAM 11-3
Streak Zone Flanker Side

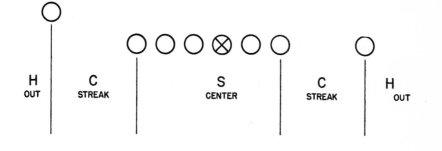

DIAGRAM 11-4
5-Deep vs. Pro

A Pro formation can open up two additonal Streak zones. Thus, we drop both corners to cover these additional zones, which gives us a 5-deep secondary (Diagram 11-4).

The corner to the split end or flanker side will drop back five yards, splitting the distance between the split receiver and the tight receiver, and keying the split receiver for a possible Look-In pass first. If there is no Look-In pass, he will back-pedal deep into the Streak zone, keying both the split receiver and the tight receiver (tight end or halfback) to his side. If the split receiver breaks out first the corner will get deep into his Streak zone, anticipating a possible Post pattern inside. If the split receiver does not break inside, the corner will look for the near back or tight end to run a deep Streak pass into his zone.

Halfback must cover the split receiver man-to-man in the Out zone both short and deep, using the pass defense techniques described in Chapter 14.

The safety's pass coverage within his Center zone versus split formations is identical to his coverage as previously described for a tight formation.

COACHING MAN-TO-MAN PASS COVERAGES

Some coaches prefer to use man-to-man pass defense versus Drop-Back passing action. Man-to-Man coverage can be easily incorporated within all of the secondary alignments included

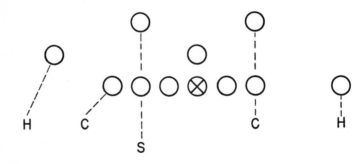

DIAGRAM 11-5
5-Deep Man-to-Man vs. Pro

within this text, and it blends quite well with the 5-deep secondary alignment.

When going to man-to-man coverage, the secondary follows our basic rules of coverage. The halfbacks take the widest receiver outside. The monsters or corners pick up the second receiver to the inside, and the safety man picks up the third receiver to the inside, which is usually the fullback.

We like to use man-to-man pass defensive coverage in conjunction with our attacking defenses, as previously described. (See Diagram 11-5 for our man-to-man 5-deep secondary versus a Pro formation.)

COACHING COMBINATION PASS COVERAGES

On occasion it is necessary to combine our basic zone, man-to-man, and double-pass coverages. Combination coverages provide the flexibility to design tailor-made pass coverages geared to meet the specific strengths and weaknesses of an offensive opponent. The following information will explain how we organize our combination coverages.

Coordinated Zone-Man-to-Man Coverage

When we call this coverage, we would call either a Zone-Right Man-Left or a Man-Right Zone-Left. Versus a Flip-Flop team, we

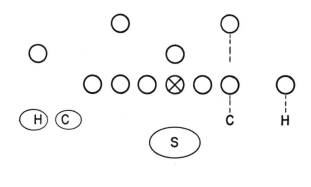

DIAGRAM 11-6
Zone-Left Man-Right

would call Zone or Man to either the Flanker or Split End side, depending upon the coverage desired. For example, we could call a Zone-to-Flanker Man-to-Split End.

The safety is always included to the side of the Zone call along with the corner and halfback to this side. The halfback and corner would employ Man coverages to the side of the Man call (Diagram 11-6).

Coordinated Zone Double Coverage

Since our loose Double coverage and our Zone coverage, as previously described, are basically the same, the Double combination coverage will pertain to our Tight Double coverage.

We would use the Tight Double coverage to take away a favorite pass pattern from a split receiver. The corner and halfback to the side of the Double call would execute the Tight Double techniques as described in Chapter 14. The call could be Zone-Left Tight-Double-Right or Zone-Right Tight-Double-Left (Diagram 11-7).

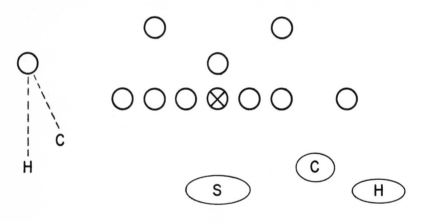

DIAGRAM 11-7
Zone-Right Tight-Double-Left

Coordinated Double Man Coverage

For the secondary coach who prefers Man-to-Man coverage over Zone coverage, he can easily combine Man-to-Man with

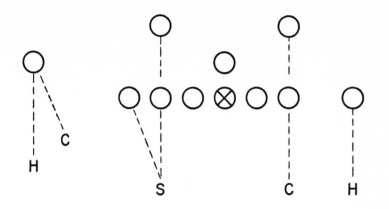

DIAGRAM 11-8
Man-Right Tight-Double Left

Double coverage instead of with Zone coverage. This coverage gives the secondary the advantage of using Double coverage and still covering the other three receivers, who are normally covered in the 4-deep with Man-to-Man coverage. The Double coverage always pertains to the corner and the halfback to the same side, thus the safety is included in the Man coverage with the opposite corner and halfback (Diagram 11-8).

PART IV

HOW TO COACH FUNDAMENTAL TECHNIQUES FOR THE 53 MULTIPLE DEFENSE

12

Establishing the Stance and Play
of Defensive Tackles and Ends

COACHING DEFENSIVE STANCE

We teach defensive tackles to align in a 3-point stance, and the defensive ends are taught to align in either a 3-point or a 2-point stance.

The coaching points that we stress for the 3-point stance are as follows:

1. The head is set down into the shoulders and looking up.
2. The shoulders are parallel to the line of scrimmage in a square alignment with neither shoulder point higher or lower than the other.
3. The back should be perfectly flat.
4. The arm that is on the same side as the staggered foot is straight down to the ground and the opposite arm is dangling down in front of the knee in a slightly crooked position with the fist clenched.
5. The hand of the supporting arm is in contact with the ground. We use a tripod position with the thumb and first two fingers bent so the weight is on the knuckles between the first and second joint.
6. The feet should be shoulder width apart with a toe-heel stagger. Long-legged men can use a slightly wider base and longer stance. However, the base or stagger must

not be exaggerated. We like a balanced stance with the body weight evenly distributed over the toe of the staggered foot, the ball of the up foot, and the knuckles of the down hand.

The coaching points that we stress for the 2-point stance are as follows:

1. The head and shoulders are parallel to the line of scrimmage, and the back is straight up from the waist and directly aligned over the balls of the feet. We do not want the body weight too far forward.
2. The knees are slightly bent in a flexed position with the front foot forward and the outside foot back in a toe-heel stagger shoulder width apart. The body weight is evenly distributed over the balls of both feet.
3. The arms are extended out in front of the body with the hands in a boxer-type stance. From this stance our ends can use their hands quickly to shed through the helmet of the tight end or weak-side tackle to the split end side.

The 3-point stance is used by interior linemen to control the inside running attack, and the 2-point stance is used by defensive ends when they are assigned to contain the outside running game through a Control technique.

COACHING THE PINCH AND SLANT TECHNIQUES

To properly execute the Pinch or Slant techniques, the interior linemen must align in a 3-point stance twelve inches off the line of scrimmage. We teach the same technique for both the Pinch and Slant techniques. The object of our technique is to get our defensive linemen into an offensive gap as quickly as possible. To accomplish this goal, we teach the lead step technique in preference to the cross-over step technique, as we feel that this technique is the quicker of the two. The coaching points that we stress for this technique are as follows:

1. On the snap of the ball, the linemen push hard off on their far foot and step with their near foot at a 45

degree angle into the near gap. As they push off on their far foot, they must bring up their far arm into an Arm Lift position to protect their legs and deliver a blow.

2. Linemen continue into the near gap taking two more quick shuffle steps, staying low, keeping their hips and shoulders parallel to the line of scrimmage, and getting their arms and hands extended out into a shedding position.

3. Throughout their shuffle movement linemen must not cross their legs, turn their bodies to the side, or penetrate the line of scrimmage, as these moves will cause them to lose balance and stability.

One of our favorite drills to teach this technique is a 2 on 1 drill. Each defensive man sets up against two offensive blockers, as shown in Diagram 12-1. The coach will station himself behind the defensive player and facing the offensive blockers. On a signal from the coach, one of the blockers moves out to block the defensive man as he moves into the gap. The defensive man never knows which blocker will block him, and he must prepare to meet either blocker on the move, shed him, and then slide away from the blocker.

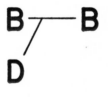

COACH

DIAGRAM 12-1
2 on 1 Drill

COACHING THE ATTACK TECHNIQUE

To execute the Attack technique, defensive linemen must again align in a 3-point stance. However, we move them back off the line of scrimmage two feet. Since the linemen are going to penetrate across the line of scrimmage on the Attack technique, we believe that by dropping them off the line of scrimmage they can gain more momentum as they attack, and it is difficult for offensive blockers to lunge out and make initial contact on the defensive linemen from this distance. We coach the Attack technique as follows:

1. On the snap of the ball, the defensive linemen will push off of their far foot and take a quick lead step that is lateral and parallel to the line of scrimmage. On this step they will bring up their far arm into an Arm Lift position.
2. As they plant their near foot on their first step, they will take a second step with their far foot at a 90 degree angle up into the near gap. Linemen must be low with their hips and shoulders parallel to the line of scrimmage. Their arms must be extended with their hands in position to shed offensive blockers.
3. On their third and fourth steps, they will penetrate across the line of scrimmage, under control, with short choppy steps. As soon as the Attack men get across the line of scrimmage they must level off, locate the football, and then take the proper lines of pursuit. The most common mistake is to over-penetrate and then chase the ball carrier from behind.

We drill our Attack technique by placing the interior linemen over offensive blockers, place mats, or dummies. The blockers or dummies are three feet apart, with a ten yard restraining line outside of the last dummy. A ball carrier is stationed five yards behind the line of scrimmage behind an offensive center. On a signal from the coach the ball carrier will move laterally and the turn up into one of the offensive holes, between the offensive blockers or to the outside of the last blocker, as directed. The defensive linemen will attack the inside gaps between the offensive blockers, level off, and then pursue the ball carrier. Linemen must attempt to square-up on the ball carrier and then two-hand-touch him. We do not gang tackle on this drill because of the lack of protection for the ball carrier. The back side linemen are instructed not to chase, but to level off and then pursue on a proper angle down-field (Diagram 12-2).

In the beginning, it is best not to use any blockers in this drill. But as the linemen progress and learn this technique, a good variation is to signal offensive linemen to block the Attack men from different angles as they move into this technique.

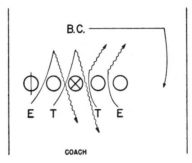

DIAGRAM 12-2
Attack Drill

COACHING THE LOOP TECHNIQUE

The Loop technique is initiated exactly like the Attack technique, as the first two steps are identical in both techniques. The only difference is that instead of penetrating across the line of scrimmage the lineman will step up to meet the near offensive lineman on the line of scrimmage, using a Control charge technique. We consider this technique a containing charge rather than a penetrating charge. A good drill that we use to teach this technique is to align the defensive men in a line at the end of a 7-man blocking sled. On a signal by the coach the first man in line will move into a Loop charge, stepping up to use a Control charge (Rip-up or 2-hand shiver) on the first pad, recoil, and then slide into another Loop charge while using a Control charge into the second pad. This procedure is repeated until each lineman has moved through all seven pads. As soon as the first man has moved on to the second pad, the next man in line will move into a Loop charge with the rest of the men in line taking their turn. As this drill progresses several men will be going at the same time, as the linemen move down the 7-man sleds in unison.

COACHING THE CONTROL TECHNIQUE

We prefer to teach the Rip-up technique for high school football players as opposed to the 2-hand shiver. If a player has tremendously strong forearms and wrists, however, we will allow him to use the 2-hand shiver. We coach the rip-up as follows:

1. From a 3-point stance, linemen will step up with their back foot. As they step up, they must bring their corresponding hand and arm up from the ground. The arm should swing as a part of the shoulder, in a slightly bent position and not at a 90 degree angle. The forearm takes the blow and the whole arm acts as a lever.
2. The forearm should be directed at the numbers of the offensive blocker, and the opposite hand should be used as added protection by driving it just under the shoulder pad of the offensive man.
3. As contact is made, the defensive man should follow through with the forearm, raising the opponent and keeping him away from his body.

This technique is used as a containing technique along the line of scrimmage. We like to teach this technique through a 1 on 1 drill with a ball carrier. This drill, which is used by most football coaches, is shown in Diagram 12-3.

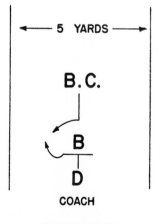

DIAGRAM 12-3

COACHING SHEDDING AND BLOCK
PROTECTION TECHNIQUES

We are sold on our Head-Hunter position technique, and we apply our basic Head-Hunter principle throughout all of our block protection techniques. The basic thinking behind this Head-Hunter principle is that we believe we must effectively counter the basic principle behind offensive blocking. This principle states that offensive blockers must get their head and body between the man they are blocking and the ball carrier. We counter this offensive principle through our Head-Hunter position technique by coaching our defensive men to read the position of the blocker's head and step into a position of advantage so the blocker cannot get his head between him and the ball carrier.

Another important fundamental of offensive blocking is that the blocker must have excellent body balance and position as he steps up to make contact with a defensive man. His shoulders must be square, with his head up and his tail down. Again, through our Head-Hunter position technique, we attempt to force the blocker into poor body balance. This can be done through the Head-Hunter technique, as we have found that the blocker's body will instinctively follow the path of his head. After the defensive man has gained a position of advantage on the blocker's head, he will attempt to force the blocker's head either to the inside or outside, causing him to lose stability and body balance.

In conjunction with our Head-Hunter position technique, we use the Arm Lift, Forearm Block, and the Hand Swipe block protection techniques.

As previously indicated, the Arm Lift technique is used in conjunction with the first and second steps of the Pinch and Slant techniques. As the linemen push off of their far foot and step with their lead leg, they will bring up their far arm from the ground, keeping this arm between their legs and the blocker. If the offensive blocker attempts to block down on the defender in the direction of his charge, he must come up underneath the blocker with his Arm Lift, driving through his head, as he moves into the near gap. By driving through the blocker's head to the inside, the blocker's body will follow. The heel of the opposite hand, near hand in the direction of the charge, is driven through the helmet or the inside shoulder of the blocker in hand shiver fashion to further turn the body of the blocker. If the defensive lineman is successful in executing this technique, he will destroy the offensive block and stack up the blocker in the running lane to cause a great deal of congestion along the line of scrimmage.

The Forearm Block is used by a slanting, pinching, or attacking lineman who has successfully moved into an offensive gap. In this situation, the Forearm Block is used to gain an inside advantage over an offensive blocker. This technique can be used by a containing defensive end who is aligned on the outside shoulder of a tight end or a weak-side tackle to the split end side. The defensive end would use this technique to gain an outside advantage over the offensive blocker.

As the defensive lineman moves into an offensive gap and he notes that an offensive blocker is attempting to drive his head and body in front of him, he will step to the inside of the blocker's head, get into a low hitting position, step with his near leg and at the same time drive his near forearm at the juncture of the shoulder and neck and then follow through the helmet, to drive the head outside. At the same time, the defender will take his far hand and grab the near arm or shoulder of the blocker in an attempt to turn his body into the hold. Through this technique, linemen can protect themselves, defend their territory, and destroy the offensive block.

From a 2-point stance the containing end would execute the Forearm Block as follows. On the snap of the ball, he will jab-step with his front foot and direct a Forearm Block at the offensive lineman. If the offensive lineman blocks down to the inside, the end will slide a step to the inside. He must not penetrate, staying parallel to the line of scrimmage in a good hitting position. From this position he must key the near back, on-side tackle, and on-side guard for a possible trap block. If the offensive lineman tries to Reach Block the defensive end to the outside, he must maintain outside leverage by staying on the outside shoulder of the blocker. This can be done by reading the blocker's head to the outside and then releasing to the outside by stepping outside with his back foot. From this position he will give ground to the outside grudgingly in an attempt to string out the play to the sidelines.

The Hand Swipe technique is used to gain an outside advantage on an offensive blocker. After the defensive lineman has successfully moved into an offensive gap and he notes that an offensive blocker is attempting to get his head behind him to gain an outside advantage, he will drop-step around the blocker's head, stepping laterally. As the lineman steps around the blocker, he will drive his outside hand (heel of hand) through the helmet of the blocker, turning the blocker's body to the inside. The opposite hand is used in conjunction with the Hand Swipe to help turn the blocker's body. As the defensive lineman steps around the blocker, he must strive to get to the outside shoulder of the blocker. The step around and Hand Swipe should be simultaneous movements.

If a blocker gets a good Reverse Shoulder block to cut off a defensive lineman, he should use a Hand Swipe and then step around him in moving towards the ball carrier. If the defender is cut off so completely that he cannot drop step around the blocker or successfully use the Hand Swipe technique, we teach him to spin out away from the blocker to the back side, and then take the proper line of pursuit downfield.

COACHING GOAL LINE TECHNIQUE

We coach a 4-point stance on the goal line. The feet should be well up in and under the body, bringing them closer to the line of scrimmage. The shoulders are down with the tail up. The weight is forward over the knuckles of both down hands, with a bend in the elbows. As the defender grabs forward into the inside gap, the shoulders are driven forward with a slight dipping action, attempting to get under the shoulders of the offensive blocker. Once under the blocker, the defender will push up with his arms and lift the blocker as he drives through for penetration to the inside. He must strive to keep his legs up under his body as he continues on his course.

We like to use a Rope Drill to teach our defensive linemen to stay low. This drill is organized by tying a rope to each end of the goal posts. The height of the rope is determined by placing all linemen in a 4-point stance and then determining which man's back is the highest. The rope is then tied to the goal posts at this height. If defensive linemen get too high, they will get stung by the rope. All of our basic defensive techniques for linemen can be practiced under the rope through a 5 on 7 drill as shown in Diagram 12-4.

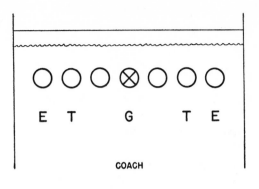

DIAGRAM 12-4

COACHING PASS RUSH TECHNIQUES

We do not go into elaborate detail in teaching many Pass Rush techniques at the high school level. However, there are some important guidelines or principles that we use in developing our basic techniques, as follows:

1. The pass rusher must align closer to the offensive blocker, six inches off the line of scrimmage, so that he can move in on the blocker in a hurry, not giving him as much time to set up for pass protection.
2. The pass rusher must move toward the passer, getting rid of the blocker on the move, and not moving laterally to get to the passer.
3. The pass rusher must attempt to destroy the body balance and stability of the blocker by forcing his body weight either forward or perpendicular to the line of scrimmage.
4. If the blocker's body weight is too far forward or he is lunging on his block, the pass rusher will pull him forward and down, step around him to the inside, and then rush the passer.
5. If the blocker presents a wing with his elbows extended out to either side of his body, the pass rusher will grab a

wing and then turn the blocker perpendicular to the line of scrimmage. Ideally, he should take the inside route. If the blocker has a good inside position, the pass rusher will have to take the outside route.

6. If the blocker is not moving his feet or if he has slow reaction, the pass rusher will sprint by him to the inside using quickness and speed.

7. If the blocker has a good inside position and he is using good pass-blocking technique, the pass rusher will use a head and shoulder fake to the inside to lure him inside, and then step around him to the outside in conjunction with the Hand Swipe technique. Through the use of the Hand Swipe to the outside of the blocker's helmet, the defender should be able to turn the blocker's body perpendicular to the line of scrimmage and beat him to the outside.

We like to drill the pass rush with just our linemen through a 5 on 7 drill or 4 on 6 drill, or we include the linebackers and drill the pass rush through a 6 on 6 or a 6 on 7 drill. During these drills the offensive blockers must set up in pass protection blocking, and the defensive linemen and linebackers must utilize their pass rush techniques and try to get past the blockers. We use either a coach or a quarterback to align behind the blockers as a passer. We insist that the pass rushers get their hands up high, to block the pass, as soon as the quarterback puts the ball up to pass. If the passer gets the ball off, the pass rushers must fly back to the ball in position to block for secondary man in case of an interception.

COACHING LINES OF PURSUIT

We never want our defensive linemen to go around the back side of a blocker and then chase the ball carrier from behind. Our linemen are taught to level off, locate the football, and then take the proper lines of pursuit according to the speed and position of the ball carrier. If the ball carrier has good speed to the outside, a back side lineman away from the flow of the football will have to take a deep angle of pursuit. A defensive lineman to the same side as the flow of the football can take a shallow angle of pursuit. The proper pursuit angle is a path that will put the defender in position to cut off the ball carrier downfield. We like to use a 5 on 7 or a 6 on 7 Pursuit Drill. A ball carrier is aligned five yards deep behind an offensive center. On a signal by a coach the center snaps the ball to the ball carrier. The ball carrier sprints laterally to a position ten yards outside of the tight end before turning upfield. The defensive linemen execute their defensive technique and then they move back towards the ball carrier, taking the proper lines of pursuit. Each defender must two-hand-touch the ball carrier at the proper point downfield (Diagram 12-5).

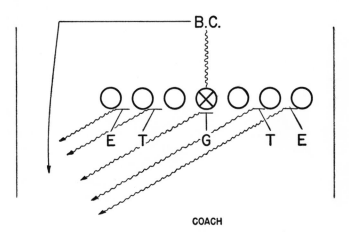

DIAGRAM 12-5
Pursuit Drill

COACHING TACKLING TECHNIQUES

Before we teach tackling, we coach our players how to assume the proper hitting position, as follows:

1. The feet should be parallel, shoulder width apart, and directly aligned under the body with the body weight evenly distributed over the balls of both feet. The feet move quickly through short choppy steps.
2. The knees are slightly bent in a flexed position.
3. The back and upper body are straight from the waist up.
4. The shoulders and upper body are square and parallel to the line of scrimmage.

5. The hands and forearms are extended out in position to shed a blocker, or in a ready position to make a tackle.

6. The head is up with eyes open, and the defender must keep his eyes glued on the belt buckle of the ball carrier. A good ball carrier can fake out a tackle with his head and shoulders or with his legs and feet, but his mid-section or belt buckle area usually remains in place.

After learning the proper hitting position, we first teach the head-on tackle as follows. As the tackler steps up with his power foot to make contact, he will shift his vision from the belt buckle to the jersey numbers. Upon contact, the tackler's forehead should land on the ball carrier's numbers and the top of his helmet should strike the ball carrier under the chin. As the tackler steps forward to make contact, he should thrust his buttocks, hips, and lower back forward and upward in one simultaneous movement. This movement will straighten his back, keep his head up, and drive the tackler up and through the ball carrier with greater hitting power and body thrust. The hands and arms must lock around the waist of the ball carrier to grasp and control him. As contact is being made, the tackler must follow through the short explosive steps, driving the ball carrier backwards. Tackler must explode upon contact, keeping his eyes open. On a perfect tackle the defender will actually lift the ball carrier into the air and then drive him down into the turf with a great thud.

We teach the basic head-on tackle through a one-in-one form tackling drill that is used by all football coaches. Players are paired off according to size. During the drill, we expect the tackler to lift his partner up into the air upon contact. The tackler will have to use perfect technique to accomplish this feat. If his head is down with his tail, he will not be able to properly execute the form tackle.

13

Toughening Defensive Middle Guard and Linebacker Play

COACHING DEFENSIVE STANCE

As previously indicated, the Power linebacker becomes a Middle Guard when we go into our Odd-Double defensive alignment. Thus, he must learn a 3-point stance and a linebacker stance. When aligning as a Middle Guard he uses the same 3-point stance that was described for defensive tackles and ends.

We align our linebackers (Power and Quick) two yards off the line of scrimmage in a 2-point stance. This stance is identical to the 2-point stance as previously described for defensive ends. We want the outside foot slightly staggered, toe-instep, so that both linebackers can release to the outside quickly to cover short passes. We have our linebackers extend their hands and forearms in a boxer stance, as we teach them to use their hands and forearms in shedding blockers on the move.

On an Even-Tight-Pro defensive call, the Power linebacker moves to the outside shoulder of the tight end. From this position, he will assume the exact 2-point stance that was described for defensive ends.

MIDDLE GUARD PLAY

The Middle Guard will use the exact same defensive techniques as described for defensive tackles and ends. He must be able to properly execute the Pinch, Slant, Attack, Loop, and

Control techniques, and he will use the same Head-Hunter position technique and the Block Protection techniques such as the Arm Lift, Forearm Block and Hand Swipe. The middle guard must be the most agile of all the defensive linemen, as he must be able to support the middle linebacker through quick lateral movement in either direction.

COACHING LINEBACKER PURSUIT
AND BLOCK PROTECTION

Because our basic defense is a moving defense, linebackers are assigned to move into an area vacated by a defensive lineman, and in most cases they will key and move with the flow of the football. Thus, our linebackers must "read" on the move, as previously described, and they must be prepared to shed blockers coming down on them from either an inside or an outside angle. Linebackers are taught to move on the snap of the ball, read the flow of the football, and then shuffle laterally as they keep themselves parallel to the line of scrimmage. We do not want them to turn their body to the side and run.

Through split vision and defensive instinct, they must see and feel an offensive blocker coming down on them and they must use the Head-Hunter position technique. If the linebacker is filling an inside gap, he will step up inside the offensive blocker's head and use a tough Forearm Block to turn his head and body to the outside. Through this technique, he can maintain an inside position to defend his assigned territory or offensive gap.

If a linebacker is pursuing an outside running play or an offensive blocker has him cut off at an inside gap through a well-executed reverse shoulder or body block, the linebacker is instructed to Drop-Step around the blocker coming down on him while using the Hand Swipe technique. Through this technique the linebacker can drive the blocker's head and body to the inside as he steps around him to the outside.

It is very important that the linebacker sheds an offensive blocker on the move. Through this approach he will get rid of the blocker as he pursues the ball carrier. A common mistake that many linebackers make is to waste valuable time trying to drive through the blocker with a shedding technique before attempting to get outside to meet a ball carrier. As a result, the ball carrier is gone and the linebacker has lost that important step or two that could have made the difference between a two-yard gain and a touchdown. The only exception to this rule is when a linebacker meets a blocker head-on. In this instance, he would use a Rip-up technique and then slide laterally to meet the ball carrier.

We use a Fill Drill to coach the proper lateral pursuit and filling technique to linebackers. We place seven dummies or mats along the line of scrimmage about three yards apart with a restraining line five yards outside of the last dummy or mat. We use two ball carriers and two linebackers in this drill at the same time. On a signal by the coach, the ball carriers will move laterally and then turn up into one of the three holes between the dummies. The linebackers must move laterally, staying one step behind the ball carrier to their side, and then mirror the movement of their offensive back by filling into the same hole to butt the ball carrier (Diagram 13-1).

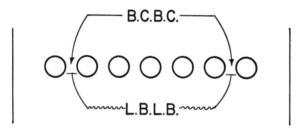

COACH

DIAGRAM 13-1
Fill Drill

COACHING LINEBACKERS TO ATTACK

Linebackers use the same Attack technique that was described for defensive linemen. However, it is very important to stress the fact that they square off and move up into an offensive gap at a 90 degree angle. There is a tendency for linebackers to hurry to cut down their attacking angle. From a squared-off position with their shoulders parallel to the line of scrimmage, they should also keep their lower body parallel to the line of scrimmage. This parallel stance will place the linebacker in an excellent position to meet blockers coming at him from either direction and, from this position, the linebacker can easily adjust his course to his right or left after penetrating across the line of scrimmage. It is very difficult for a linebacker to control his body and change direction when attacking on a sharp angle across the line of scrimmage.

Linebackers use the same Attacking Drill that was illustrated for defensive linemen. They can work on this drill alone or they can work with the defensive linemen as a Forcing Unit.

COACHING BODY BALANCE AND HITTING TECHNIQUE

First, we teach linebackers how to get into the proper hitting position as previously described. In order for our linebackers to execute our hitting technique, they must have excellent body balance at all times. We like to teach linebackers how to maintain good body balance on the move through a Mirror Drill. Two men pair off with one man as a ball carrier and the other man as a linebacker. These men work in a five-yard square. The ball carrier will move forward two steps and then laterally make two more cuts from side to side. The linebacker will mirror the movement of the ball carrier by moving up two steps and then sliding laterally with the ball carrier as he makes his fakes. The linebacker must move his feet with quick, short, and choppy steps, with his body weight evenly distributed over the balls of his feet. As the ball carrier moves laterally, the linebacker must strive to maintain a parallel head-up position directly in front of the ball carrier (Diagram 13-2).

We teach Head-Hunter and shedding techniques to linebackers through a Machine Gun Drill. A linebacker assumes a hitting position facing three offensive blockers. On a signal by the coach one of the three blockers will attack the defensive man. The offensive men are signaled to move one after another in rapid-fire succession; however, the coach will give the linebacker time to get set before signaling the next blocker. If the middle blocker moves out on the linebacker, he will use a Rip-up technique. If one of the outside blockers moves down on the linebacker, he will read the blocker's head and then use either a Forearm Block or a Hand Swipe technique (Diagram 13-3).

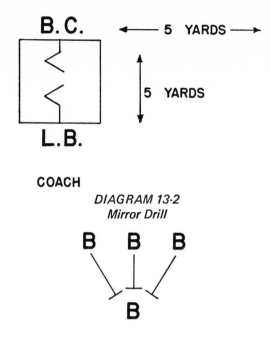

COACH

DIAGRAM 13-2
Mirror Drill

COACH

DIAGRAM 13-3
Machine Gun Drill

We believe that a defensive football player must learn to use his forehead effectively in executing the proper hitting technique while tackling. In the beginning, we like to use the Crowther 7-Man sled to teach the proper use of the helmet and forehead. We align the linebackers at the end of the sled. The first man steps up and aims his forehead and helmet, with his head and neck in a bull neck position, at the lower level just under the T-pad. As he steps up to make contact, he brings his hands up to lift the sled at the same time. The first man will drop-step and then slide laterally to make contact with the second T-pad. Each man will take a turn, one after another, moving down the length of the sled until each man has made contact with all seven T-pads. Defensive linemen also use this drill.

The next hitting drill that we use is a One-on-One Hitting Drill. The two men are five yards apart. The coach rolls a football on the ground to the ball carrier and he attempts to run straight ahead through the linebacker. As soon as the ball carrier picks up the ball, the linebacker will move straight into him using the proper hitting technique. We butt in this drill instead of tackle. However, everything else about the body position and hitting technique is identical to our form tackle as previously described for defensive linemen. We encourage tough contact with both men going all out in this drill. The ball carrier makes no attempt to fake the linebacker out of position (Diagram 13-4).

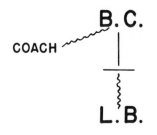

DIAGRAM 13-4
One-on-One Hitting Drill

After linebackers have learned to hit and maintain good body balance, we put them through a Butt Drill. This drill combines both body balance and hitting technique, and it is organized exactly like the Mirror Drill, the only difference being that the width of the area is ten yards instead of five yards.

The ball carrier will move towards the linebacker, making two or three cuts or fakes in opposite directions. He will then utilize the entire ten yard width and try to outrun the linebacker to the outside. The linebacker must move into a good hitting position and mirror the moves of the ball carrier. After mirroring the first two cuts, the linebacker will attempt to square-up with the ball carrier and use a butting technique with his forehead on the numbers. The hands are placed out in front of the body in a pushing position, and the linebacker will lift the ball carrier with his hands as he butts him with his head. He will thrust his lower body as if he were tackling (Diagram 13-5).

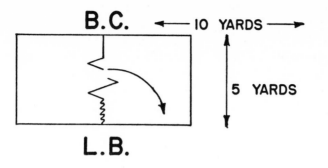

COACH

DIAGRAM 13-5
Butt Drill

We stress neck exercises daily in preparation for our hitting drills. We use neck bridging and isometric neck exercises each day before we begin practice. These exercises must be done daily if the defensive coach stresses the use of the forehead and helmet through Hitting Drills.

PASS DEFENSIVE TECHNIQUES
FOR LINEBACKERS

Pass defense techniques for linebackers were covered in detail in Chapter 8, so it is not necessary to repeat that material. However, we do want to stress the fact that it is important that the defensive coach organize his schedule so that the linebackers will drill with the defensive secondary versus the passing game.

We use a Unit Recognition Drill with the linebackers, corners, halfbacks, and the safety man working against a skeleton offensive unit that includes a tight end, split end, and four offensive backs. With a center snapping the ball to a quarterback, this drill becomes a seven-on-seven drill. The offensive unit will align in various offensive sets, and they will run all of the varied types of passes, such as drop-back (screen and draw), roll-out, play-action pass, and bootleg or throw-back passes. The defensive unit must call out the name of the formation, adjust to the formation, and then key and cover the specific offensive play action. We stress the fact that the entire unit must call out the specific name of the offensive play action, such as "Pass" or "Roll-Out." Once the ball is in the air the entire unit must fly to the ball.

14

Putting Into Shape
Defensive Secondary Play

COACHING DEFENSIVE STANCE

Versus a tight offensive formation, defensive corners and halfbacks assume the same defensive stance. This stance is identical to the 2-point stance previously described for containing defensive ends. On occasion, defensive corners move up to align on the outside shoulder of a tight end. Again, in this instance they must align in the 2-point containing position.

This same 2-point stance is used for corners aligned in their normal corner alignment and for defensive halfbacks aligned in their basic halfback alignment. The outside foot is back so that corners and halfbacks can open-up fast to the outside in order to cover their Flat and deep One Third zones. The weight should be equally distributed over the balls of both feet, with the toes angling slightly to the inside. From this position they can face to the inside and key through the tight end to the near back and quarterback.

Halfbacks align two yards outside of a split receiver. In this situation, we alter their stance by placing their inside foot back and their outside foot forward. This change is made so that the halfback can face to the inside in a better position to see through the split receiver to the quarterback. We have found that it is very difficult for the halfback to see through to the quarterback from a wide position with his outside foot back. This, of course, is not true in a tight formation. Also, from this stance versus a split receiver, he is in excellent position to run backwards immediately if the split receiver releases straight down the field at top speed. This is true because he has opened up to the inside with his inside foot back and it is not necessary for him to pivot back into this position before running.

If the receiver is eight yards or closer to the sideline, halfbacks will assume a normal stance with their outside foot back, using the sideline as an extra man.

With our secondary aligned in a 3-deep, the defensive safety aligns in a 2-point stance from eight to fifteen yards deep, depending upon the game situation. He will normally align in a 2-point stance with both feet parallel, as he must be prepared to open-up to either side according to the flow of the football. If the safety feels more comfortable with either foot back, we will allow him to alter his stance accordingly. At times, we believe it is wise for the safety to open-up his outside foot to the wide side of the field or to the strength of the offensive formation such as a Slot, Flanker, or Spread.

COACHING RUNNING BACKWARDS
TECHNIQUES

Because we teach zone pass defensive coverage as our basic pass coverage, we stress the Running Backwards technique as opposed to the Back Pedal technique. However, defensive corners will use the Back Pedal technique during their first few steps against a split receiver. We coach the Running Backwards technique as follows:

A good pass defender must master the art of running backwards. From his waist down he must turn and run at top speed while from his waist up he must be parallel to the line of scrimmage so that he faces through the pass receiver to the quarterback. This technique of turning the lower body and running will allow the defender to sprint at top speed, which is a necessity in covering a fast receiver. Also, this technique of turning the upper body to face through the receiver to the quarterback will enable the secondary to follow the flight of the ball as it leaves the quarterback's hand. The fundamentals of this technique are essential to the successful execution of our zone pass defense.

A good defender must be able to change direction while on the run and still maintain visual contact with the receiver and quarterback at all times. For example, if a defender must change direction to his left while running to his right, he must plant his back foot (right foot), lower his body, pivot on the planted foot, roll his hips, and change direction from right to left. The opposite would be true when changing direction to his left. Two unforgivable sins are turning his back to the receiver and passer or crossing his back foot over his front foot while changing direction instead of planting the back foot and pivoting back as described above. It is impossible, in our opinion, for our secondary man to properly execute zone pass coverage if he loses visual contact with the receiver and the ball or allows his legs to get tangled up.

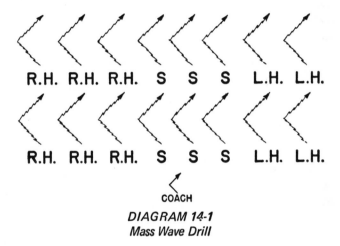

R.H. R.H. R.H.   S   S   S   L.H. L.H.

R.H. R.H. R.H.   S   S   S   L.H. L.H.

COACH

DIAGRAM 14-1
Mass Wave Drill

We teach the basic Running Backwards technique through the Mass and Unit Wave drills.

The Mass Wave Drill is used to teach large numbers of secondary men how to run backwards properly. The backs are aligned about three yards apart in width and depth. Right halfbacks and corner men will have their right foot back and left halfbacks and corner men will have their left foot back. The safety will be aligned in a parallel stance between the halfbacks and corner men to either side of him. The coach stands mid-way between the secondary men, facing the safety men. With a football in his hand he will fake a passing motion to his right or left. As soon as the coach puts the ball up, the secondary will yell "pass" and then turn and run in the direction of the fake pass. They must keep their eyes glued on the passer at all times while executing the proper running footwork. The coach will fake the passing motion several times to his right and left so that the defensive backs will have to change direction several times. If the coach fakes a pass motion straight ahead, secondary men will back pedal, and if he pulls the ball straight back towards himself, the secondary men return to their original positions (Diagram 14-1).

The Unit Wave Drill is exactly like the Mass Wave Drill except that a single defensive unit is used instead of a mass group of players.

COACHING PASS DEFENSIVE
TECHNIQUES

When covering a pass receiver to the outside in the Flat or Out zones, the defensive corner and halfback must always maintain a position of two yards in width and three yards in depth from an offensive receiver. The purpose of this is to give the secondary an advantage in width and depth which makes it very difficult for the receiver to beat him either to his outside or deep. When covering a split receiver in the Out zone, the halfback is responsible for covering the split receiver both long and short. Thus, by following the above rules in width and depth, the halfback can prevent the split receiver from beating him short or deep.

When covering the inside zones, such as the corner's coverage of the Streak zone versus a split receiver or the safety's coverage of the Center zone versus a tight end, both men must observe the same three-yard rule in depth and two-yard rule in width from the offensive receiver. As the receiver moves into the inside Streak or Center zones, the secondary man must move into a position slightly to the inside shoulder of the receiver while still maintaining the three yards in depth. From this inside position, the secondary must maintain a parallel position so that he can see the receiver and the quarterback through split vision at the same time. Thus he will see the initial flight of the ball and will be in position to play through the receiver from the inside position. In theory and play this inside position and coverage is identical to the outside coverage.

The next fundamental rule for secondary men in their execution of zone pass defense is that they should never commit themselves until the ball is in the air. If they commit too soon, they will lose their two yards in width and their three yards in depth ratio from the receiver and the receiver can easily beat them on any up- or go- type of pass pattern.

Talking is a very important technique when using zone pass defensive coverage. Secondary men must continuously communicate with each other. This is particularly true when using the Switch technique along with combination pass coverages.

First, our secondary men must recognize the offensive formation and then call it out loud and clear. Second, they must recognize the offensive play action and then call out this action immediately upon recognition.

When utilizing zone pass defense, secondary men must first yell "pass" as soon as they recognize drop-back pass. If an outside receiver runs an inside route, we expect the outside halfback to yell "coming across John," yelling out the name of the secondary man to the inside. If two receivers on the same side run cross-type patterns, secondary men must give the "switch" call indicating that they will switch receivers coming into their respective zones. And finally, once the ball leaves the quarterback's hand, secondary men yell "ball."

The final phase of pass defense is making the interception. First, defensive backs must fly to the football at top speed regardless of which part of the field the football is thrown to. As the defender sprints to intercept the ball, he must see the football leave the quarterback's hand and then "look" the football into his hands in the same manner as an offensive receiver. Also while on the move, they must learn to judge the flight of the ball in the same manner as an outfielder in baseball. The best method of learning to judge a football in flight is practice and more practice.

When going up to intercept the pass, we want our defender to square off his hips in a position parallel to the line of scrimmage, getting good body position on the receiver (like a rebounder going up for the ball in basketball), and then catch the ball at its highest point. If the secondary back fails to carry out these interception techniques, the receiver will come back for the football and beat the defender every time. As soon as the back intercepts the ball he yells "score," as we want him to think in terms of scoring as soon as he gets his hands on the ball. We use the Mass and Unit Wave Drills to practice the interception technique. The only difference is that the coach will pass the ball for the interception instead of just faking the pass.

COACHING OUTSIDE CONTAINING TECHNIQUES

The corners and halfbacks are responsible for outside containment. To fulfill this responsibility, they are taught to rotate fast to the outside, under control, and then maneuver into a position of advantage on the outside shoulder of the first offensive blocker. From this outside position we ask secondary men to head-hunt. We follow the premise that the only way a blocker can beat our man to the outside is to allow him to get his head and body between him and the sideline. To prevent this from occurring, secondary men hunt the head and then shed through the head using a Forearm Block or a two-hand shiver to force the blocker's head inside.

When we align the defensive corner in an outside attacking position on the line of scrimmage, he will attack as follows: To the side of flow, the corner will angle to the inside at a 60 degree angle. He will take three steps across the line of scrimmage. His first and third steps are taken with his inside foot so that he can meet the first blocker with his inside or power foot, with his outside leg free to the outside. The corner should not get as deep as the first blocker as this would place him in a good position to be either trapped or kicked out with the ball carrier turning up to the inside. Rather, the corner must stay a step in front of the first blocker and the ball carrier so that he can step up to meet the blocker and be in a position to force the ball carrier deep and to the outside.

To the side of flow, if the corner is aligned in a pinching position, he will take the same three steps to the inside and on the third step prepare to make contact on the outside shoulder of the tight end or wingback. From this position, his technique and play is exactly the same as described for the containing defensive end.

When adjusting to a wingback, the corner will observe the

following rules. If the wing is in a tight alignment from 1½ to 2 yards in depth and width from the tight end, the corner will align on his outside shoulder when anticipating run. However, we will drop him off into his normal corner position when anticipating pass. From three to five yards out the corner will align head-up on the wingback or split end. The purpose of this head-up position is to take away the crack-back block. Anytime a split man is flankered out more than five yards the corner can move inside into a tight alignment versus run. We do not feel that a split man can get a good crack-back block on a quick-charging corner when he is out more than five yards.

We also teach our secondary men how to maintain good body balance and position in open field situations through the same drills and techniques that were previously described for defensive linebackers.

COACHING TACKLING TECHNIQUES

We coach and drill the head-on tackle to our secondary men in the same manner as previously described for defensive linemen.

Actually, our secondary men do more angle tackling than head-on tackling because of their outside rotation and containment in support of the outside running game. Thus, we stress angle tackling and coach this technique as follows.

On an angle tackle it is very important that the tackler drive his head and shoulders in front of and then through the ball carrier. He should aim his forehead and helmet at the far arm of the ball carrier. For this approach he will have to get his head and shoulders into the proper position. Also from this position it is possible that he can force a fumble by hitting the football with his helmet, knocking the football out of the ball carrier's arm. We have taught the roll action in conjunction on with this technique; however, we have found that this technique is not realistic in game situations. Instead, we just tell our tackles to drive the ball carrier up into the bleachers after contact is made through great leg drive and follow-through of the body.

We teach our secondary men how to shed a blocker and then make the angle tackle through our Sideline Tackling Drill. This drill is organized as follows.

An area ten yards from the sideline is marked off. This area

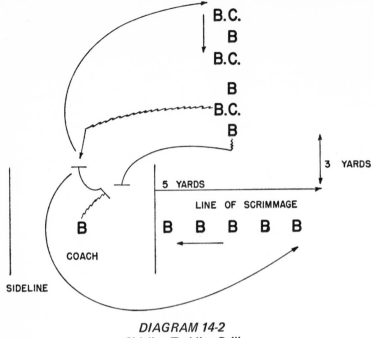

DIAGRAM 14-2
Sideline Tackling Drill

forms a lane or an alley down the sideline. It is possible to use a
chalked line or dummies to mark off this area.

A blocker and ball carrier align three yards deep and five
yards to the inside of this alley area. The defensive backs are
stationed mid-way or five yards to the inside of the alley area. On
a signal from the coach, the blocker will lead the ball carrier
around the inside corner of the alley and then down the sideline.
It is important that these offensive men turn up into the alley
immediately and not run towards the sidelines and then out of
bounds. Also, the ball carrier cannot cut to the inside of the
blocker. He must run outside of the blocker and then down the
sideline.

The defensive back must rotate up to shed the blocker and
then make the tackle. The defensive back must head-hunt and
assume the proper hitting position as he sheds through the helmet
of the blocker.

After each man in the defensive group has had two or three
tackles the two groups rotate, with the offensive men taking turns
at tackling. The coach assumes a position behind the tackler so
that he is in good position to observe the technique (Diagram
14-2).

PART V

HOW TO DESIGN 53 MULTIPLE TEAM DEFENSIVE COVERAGES

15

Defensing the Belly Series
With the 53 Multiple

The Belly Series is considered by most football experts to be one of the most deceptive offensive series in football. Coach Bobby Dodd's Georgia Tech teams popularized the Belly Series with great success during the early 1950's. During the past twenty years imaginative football coaches, through various ramifications, have developed this offensive series into a devastating attack. The most recent innovation of the Belly Series is the Belly Triple Option Play run so successfully by the Universities of Texas and Houston, and the Power T Football Series run at Oregon State University which features the Fullback Power Belly Play.

The purpose of the Belly Series is to isolate specific defensive players and then force them either to freeze or commit an error in movement. Thus the offense is able to take away from the defense the initiative to control the game.

We believe that the defense must counter this strategy by taking the initiative away from the offense. This can be done by forcing the offensive team to run the specific Belly options into the strength of a specific defensive call, taking the initiative away from the offense and making them play our game.

Various forms of the modern Belly Series are being run from every conceivable offensive formation. Also, deceptive counter plays and play action passes are being incorporated within these series of plays. Thus, today's Belly Series is extremely flexible.

How can the defense cope with such a devastating attack? Some coaches even maintain that certain forms of the Belly Series are impossible to stop. Nonsense—we believe that a flexible, well-executed defense can properly defend against any offensive series in football. The key is meeting offensive strength with defensive strength in a proportionate manner, giving the defensive men man-to-man assignments according to the offensive play action. If the defense covers every offensive back and end on each Belly play—for run and pass—they can adequately cover all of the Belly play options. We achieve this man-to-man coverage by designing specific defensive plays according to the offensive formation and anticipated play action.

The following illustrations will describe how the 53 Multiple Defense can adjust in defending against today's Belly Series of plays. It will not be necessary to elaborate on defensive techniques, as this material has been covered in detail.

INSIDE BELLY SERIES

This series is run quite successfully from the Power T running attack. This attack is run from a Split-End formation with a full-house T formation backfield. A powerful inside running game is featured to the tight end or solid-side with the onside halfback as a blocker and the fullback as an inside running threat. However, the defense m must also prepare to defend against the passing threat of the split end to the short side.

We would adjust to the tight end side by jumping our Power Corner to an Inside position so as to effectively meet the strength of the onside halfback as a blocker to the inside. We would adjust to the split end side by dropping off our Quick Corner to double-cover the split end with the defensive halfback.

It should be noted that we place the Power Corner in an inside position head-up on the tight end. The purpose of this inside alignment is to take a blocking angle away from the tight end so that he cannot block the Power Corner.

The Inside Belly Series is designed to isolate the defensive tackle and inside linebacker. They must honor the fullback run inside. If they freeze and do not commit inside, the fullback will drive inside for large chunks of yardage. If they commit inside on the fullback, the quarterback will hand off to the second back just to the outside of the defensive tackle and linebacker. An effective third option off this series is a quarterback-keep run or pass outside. Other deceptive counter plays such as an inside run, quarterback bootleg, and throw back pass to the split end can destroy a defense that pursues too fast and does not cover the back side properly.

All the Inside Belly options begin with the belly fake to the fullback. Anytime the quarterback fakes the ball inside to the fullback on Belly action, the inside linebackers and corners are coached to yell "Belly," and then the entire defensive unit must yell "Belly" and execute their man-to-man assignments according to the defensive call.

The following diagrams and man-to-man assignments will illustrate how we defend against the Inside Belly Series. Note that we move the tackle and back side linebacker to the inside shoulder in a position of advantage.

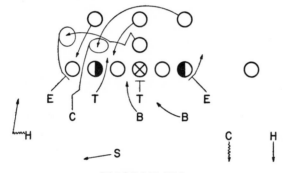

DIAGRAM 15-1
Odd-Double-Inside-Tackle-Gap

Onside Man-to-Man Assignments (Diagram 15-1)

1. Middle linebacker: Will key F.B. and tackle him
2. Tackle: Will tackle fullback
3. Power corner: Will key and tackle second back
4. End: Will jam T. E. and contain Q.B.
5. Halfback: Key pass and contain outside
6. Safety: Key pass and support run containment

The halfback and safety will key the tight end and onside halfback for Belly pass. If the tight end releases, the halfback takes

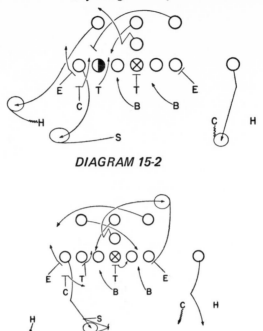

DIAGRAM 15-2

DIAGRAM 15-3
Backside Coverages

the near back man-to-man and the safety takes the tight end man-to-man (Diagram 15-2).

Backside Man-to-Man Assignments (Diagram 15-3)

1. Middle tackle: Control and key inside counter
2. Quick linebacker: Key far back for counter
3. End: Key quarterback bootleg and contain
4. Quick corner: Key near back for throw-back pass, no throw-back, key S.E. bootleg pass
5. Halfback: Key split end for throw-back or bootleg pass

We would defend against the Inside Belly Series to the split-end side in the same manner as shown in Diagram 15-4.

We would use and an Odd-Double-Pinch call as an alternate call. The defensive end and corner to the tight end side exchange assignments, with the end taking the second back through and the

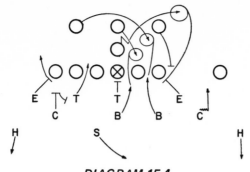

DIAGRAM 15-4
Split-End-Side-Coverage

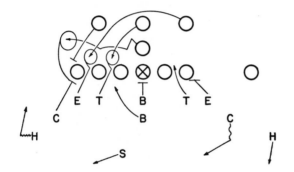

DIAGRAM 15-5
Odd-Double-Pinch

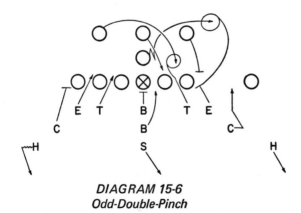

DIAGRAM 15-6
Odd-Double-Pinch

corner taking the quarterback keeper. All other assignments remain the same. Versus the Inside Belly to the split-end side, the tackle would pinch down hard on the fullback to support the middle linebacker. The end and corner would take the quarterback keeper (Diagrams 15-5 and 15-6).

We would jump our defensive unit back and forth between these two alignments to attempt to confuse the offensive blocking.

BELLY OPTION SERIES

This series is also run effectively from the Power T running attack. We will illustrate this series from the Split-End Full-House T formation. To meet offensive strength with defensive strength, we would align in the same defensive alignments that were diagrammed versus the Inside Belly Series.

The purpose of this series is to isolate the defensive end in a two-on-one situation. If he plays the pitch man the quarterback will keep inside, and if he commits on the quarterback, the quarterback will pitch to the halfback.

Most teams release their tight end to the outside on this play as a blocker or receiver. Thus, they have lost a blocker to the inside. This opens up the gates for an inside man to pressure the quarterback. Our strategy is to assign a man to pressure the quarterback, forcing him to pitch, with a second man in position to take the pitch man.

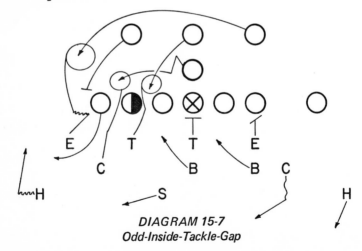

DIAGRAM 15-7
Odd-Inside-Tackle-Gap

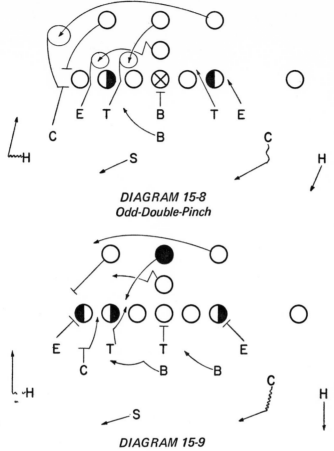

DIAGRAM 15-8
Odd-Double-Pinch

DIAGRAM 15-9
Odd-Inside-Tackle-Gap

On option key the end, corner, and halfback to the option side must yell "option" to alert them to their assignments.

On an Odd-Inside-Tackle-Gap call, the corner will take the quarterback and the end will take the pitch man. They exchange assignments on an Odd-Double-Pinch call with the end taking the quarterback and the corner taking the pitch man. An important coaching point is that the man assigned to take the pitch man must force the tight end to take an inside release through a tough Forearm Block or Hand Swipe technique. This move provides the contain man with a clear path to the pitch man.

To the split-end side, on both of the above defensive calls, the end takes the quarterback with the corner taking the pitch man.

The rest of the assignments versus the fullback inside, halfback counter, quarterback bootleg, throw back pass, and play action pass are identical as illustrated for the Inside Belly Series (Diagrams 15-7 and 15-8).

The Power T attack runs a fullback power play off tackle from their Belly Option Series. The tight end blocks down and the onside halfback kicks out. In defending against this play the defensive end must key the tight end. If he blocks down instead of releasing, he will step inside to meet the onside halfback. The power corner will step up to meet the tight end with a Rip-up from an inside position to take the fullback. The middle linebacker will slide laterally to key the fullback from an inside position (Diagram 15-9).

16

Defensing the Belly Triple Option With the 53 Multiple

BELLY TRIPLE OPTION

The Belly Triple Option is the most popular modern version of the Belly Series, and the most difficult to defend against because of the 3-way option. We adjust to this triple option by meeting offensive strength with defensive strength, with as many defensive men at the offensive point of attack as offensive men. It then becomes a matter of what kind of men make up the X's and O's, and how well they are coached in the fundamentals of football. In our opinion, there is no magic offense or defense in the game of football that is capable of completely dominating either phase of the game.

The 3-way option isolates both the defensive tackle and the end on the line of scrimmage, and simultaneously forces the defensive secondary to play pass instead of run. This places the defense in a deep freeze, giving the offense the initiative.

The quarterback's first option is to key the first man aligned outside of the offensive tackle. If he waits or comes across the line of scrimmage, the quarterback will hand off the ball to the fullback inside. If the tackle commits inside toward the fullback, the quarterback will pull the ball away from the fullback and run a split-T option on the defensive end. If the end commits on the quarterback he will pitch to the halfback or, if the end plays the pitch man, the quarterback will keep on an inside run. The tight end and flanker both release downfield so that the defensive safety and halfback will have to stay back to honor pass.

We want our defensive unit to take away the initiative from the offense. This can be done by forcing each of the 3-way options. First, we purposely align a defensive man on the outside eye or nose of the offensive tackle. The offensive tackle's job is to block either the inside gap or linebacker. Thus, from this stance the defensive tackle will not be blocked by the offensive tackle and he is free to attack the fullback inside. As he attacks inside he will drive through the head of the offensive tackle with an Arm Lift, making it difficult for him to block the linebacker. This move forces the quarterback into his second option.

From our Odd alignment, the inside linebacker will shade the outside eye of the offensive guard to get a slight advantage to the outside. This stance makes it very difficult for the offensive guard to pick up the attacking linebacker. From this position, the inside linebacker attacks the quarterback to force the second option, as shown in Diagram 16-1. This pressure forces the quarterback into his third and final option: he must pitch to the halfback.

Versus a Flanker formation as shown in Diagram 16-1, the corner is assigned to take the pitch man. The tight end is coached to release outside. It is the defensive end's job to force the tight end to release inside, as previously described. This technique frees the corner to come up on the pitch man immediately, or it will prevent the tight end from hooking the defensive end. The defensive end is then free to help either inside or outside, depending on where he is needed most.

The halfback is assigned to cover the flanker man-to-man and the safety is assigned to cover the tight end man-to-man. The safety will slide over into a safety blitz alignment in an ideal position to cover the tight end. The technique of the defensive end forcing the tight end to the inside also helps the safety in his pass coverage.

Diagrams 16-2 through 16-6 will show possible coverages versus several of the most popular formations. Note that in all of the following coverages we force the quarterback to run the outside option with two men in position to take the quarterback and pitch man. The releasing tight end and flanker are both covered man-to-man. The back side coverages are identical to those previously described.

To counter our defensive maneuver of positioning two men outside to take the quarterback and pitch men, the triple option

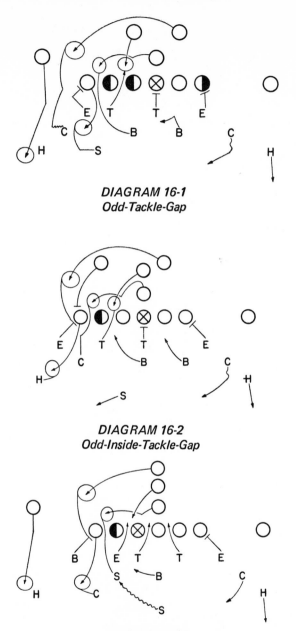

DIAGRAM 16-1
Odd-Tackle-Gap

DIAGRAM 16-2
Odd-Inside-Tackle-Gap

DIAGRAM 16-3
Even-Tight-Safety-Tackle-Gap

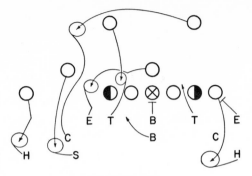

DIAGRAM 16-4
Odd-Double-Inside-Tackle-Gap

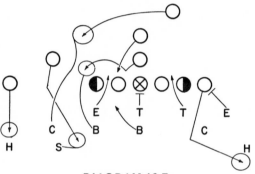

DIAGRAM 16-5
Odd-Inside-Tackle-Gap

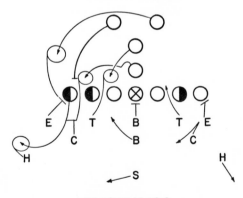

DIAGRAM 16-6
Odd-Double-Tackle-Gap

can adjust to this situation with an Outside Belly Option. The purpose of this play would be to force the defensive end to take the fullback so that the quarterback would have a two-on-one situation on the defensive corner. However, to properly execute this variation the offense must use its tight end to block to the inside. We could adjust to this outside variation in two ways. First, we could use our Odd-Tackle-Gap technique and force the tight end to block our linebacker. The safety keys the tight end man-to-man. If he blocks instead of releasing, the safety will attack the tackle-gap and take the quarterback. The end would tackle the fullback, and the corner would take the pitch man.

Another possibility would be a Slant call to the flanker. The slanting tackle would force a double-team block from the tight end and offensive tackle. This technique would free the safety to key the tight end and then attack into the tackle-gap to tackle the quarterback (Diagrams 16-7 and 16-8).

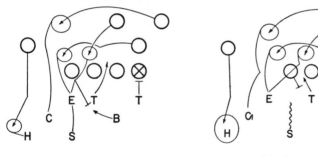

DIAGRAM 16-7
Odd-Tackle-Gap

DIAGRAM 16-8
Odd-Slant-Left

WISHBONE-T TRIPLE OPTION SERIES

The utilization of the onside halfback as a lead blocker provides the Wishbone-T version of the Triple Option with excellent outside blocking. To counter this outside blocking threat, we would use a different outside containing technique than the one described for the Houston Triple Option. As previously described, we would force the quarterback and the pitch man, which we believe is the best technique versus the triple option without a lead blocker because our two outside contain men can take the quarterback and pitch men without being blocked. However, versus the Wishbone-T Triple Option we would not force the quarterback or the pitch man. Instead, we would ask our man assigned to the quarterback to slide along the line of scrimmage, staying parallel to the quarterback and directly in front of him while maintaining a good hitting position. This man would not commit toward the quarterback or force him. Rather, he would let the quarterback make the first move and then react according to his initial movement.

Because of the split-second timing involved between the quarterback and the pitch man, the quarterback cannot afford to hesitate too long with a contain man standing directly in front of him. Instantly, at this point he must decide whether to keep or pitch. If he keeps, the assigned defender will tackle him. If he pitches, the defender will move quickly to the outside shoulder of the quarterback, putting him in an outside position of advantage in case the quarterback tries to block him. He then pursues the pitch man from an inside position to support our outside contain man.

We believe that this sliding containing technique will confuse the quarterback, since he is coached to read a forcing defensive end. Thus we can counter the quarterback's key and put our defender in the driver's seat, giving him the initiative.

The player assigned to take the pitch man will key the lead blocker or onside halfback and then jump on his outside shoulder, using our basic outside containing technique. He must not let the lead blocker or pitch man turn the outside corner (Diagram 16-9).

We would use various defensive calls as a change-up from down to down in an attempt to confuse the Wishbone-T ball handling and blocking. However, we would follow the same basic guidelines or principles within each defensive call, as follows:

1. We would definitely attempt to corral the fullback with two men from both an inside and an outside position, and we would coach these men to tackle the fullback.
2. We would assign a man to align on the outside shoulder of the tight end. This man would be coached to force the tight end to take an inside release route. This would be a must assignment.
3. We would always have three men in an outside position to take the fullback, quarterback, and pitch man on a

man-to-man basis, with two of these men outside of the tight end or the weak side tackle in position to take the quarterback and pitch man.

We would tackle the fullback to take away this portion of the triple option for three reasons. First, we must eliminate him as an inside running threat. A good fullback will eat up consistent yardage inside all day to give the offense that first-and-ten when they need it. By tackling the fullback we eliminate him as a blocker or a pass receiver.

The tight end is used as a blocker or receiver as he releases outside to remove the defensive halfback. By forcing the tight end to release to his inside at all times we eliminate him as a blocker, which frees our outside contain man to move up on the pitch man unmolested. Also, the defensive safety can easily use our 3-Rotate technique to cover a tight end taking an inside route on a pass play. Again, this frees the defensive halfback to move up outside through a 3-Rotate to either take the pitch man or cover the near back in the flat zone.

A typical game plan versus the Wishbone-T Triple Option would be devised as follows. We would use the Odd-Inside-Tackle-Gap and an Even-Split-Control as tough change-up defensive calls versus the inside running game and the outside option. To provide better outside support versus the outside option when we need it, we would call an Odd-Tackle-Gap with a safety blitz secondary call. As an adjustment to the wide side of the field we would call an Odd-Safety-Tackle-Gap, which would give us an overload effect to the wide side.

As can be seen in the following diagrams we give our interior linemen and linebackers the option of aligning either in an outside or an inside position of advantage according to the anticipated offensive play action. We change-up our outside containment so that the quarterback, pitch man, and lead blocker never know for sure whether the linebacker, corner, halfback, or safety man is going to contain them.

Odd-Inside-Tackle-Gap Assignments

1. Safety: With belly action to the tight end he must cover the tight end man-to-man, and with belly action to the split end he must slide laterally and support the quick corner from an inside position.

2. Halfbacks: Halfback to the tight end side will rotate up and contain the outside, and halfback to the split end side will cover the split end man-to-man for pass and then support run outside if he tries to block him.

3. Corners: Power corner to the tight end side will align head-up over the offensive tackle, and it is his job to key the tackle's block. If he blocks down inside, corner will slide into the Tackle-Gap and contain the quarterback by using our sliding technique. If he blocks out on our defensive tackle, corner will fill the Guard-Gap and tackle the fullback. Quick corner to the split end side will use a 4-Rotate technique and contain the outside with belly action towards him.

4. Ends: Both ends will align on the outside shoulder of the tight end and the weak side tackle. End to the tight end side will force the tight end to take an inside release route and then help contain the outside option using our sliding technique. End to the split end side will drive through the head of the offensive tackle and attempt to tackle the fullback. If tackle blocks out on end, the latter will slide laterally and contain the quarterback outside, exchanging assignments with the quick linebacker.

5. Tackles: Middle tackle will use a control charge and then cover the back side Center-Gap away from belly action for an inside counter. Strong side tackle will drive through the head of offensive tackle and attempt to tackle the fullback. If tackle blocks out on him, he will slide outside into the Tackle-Gap and contain the quarterback, exchanging assignments with power corner.

6. Linebackers: Quick backer to the split end side is aligned head-up over the offensive tackle. He will key the tackle's block. If he blocks inside, backer will use an Eagle containing technique to contain the quarterback. If he blocks out on the defensive end, backer will fill the Guard-Gap and tackle the fullback, exchanging assignments with the defensive end. Power linebacker, aligned as a middle linebacker, will key belly action and tackle the fullback from an inside position.

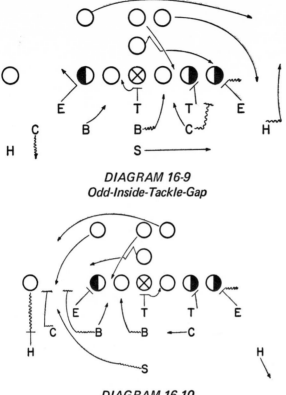

DIAGRAM 16-9
Odd-Inside-Tackle-Gap

DIAGRAM 16-10
Odd-Inside-Tackle-Gap

Even-Split-Control Assignments (See Diagrams 16-11 and 16-12).

1. Safety: Same assignments as illustrated in Diagrams 16-9 and 16-10.
2. Halfbacks: Same assignments as illustrated in Diagrams 16-9 and 16-10.
3. Corners: Quick corner has same assignments as shown in Diagrams 16-9 and 16-10. Power corner is aligned on the outside shoulder of the tight end, and he must force the tight end to release to the inside and then contain the outside option.
4. Ends: Both ends will align on the outside shoulder of the offensive tackles. They will use a control technique

and then slide into a parallel position to contain the quarterback through our sliding technique.

5. Tackles: Both tackles will align in a split alignment on the outside shoulder of the offensive guards. From this alignment they will use a control technique and attempt to tackle the fullback from an inside position.

6. Linebackers: Both linebackers will align over the Center-Gaps. To the side of belly action the linebacker will move into the Guard-Gap and tackle the fullback from an outside position. The back side linebacker will move over the offensive center and check for counter action up the middle.

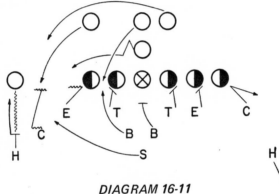

DIAGRAM 16-11
Even-Split-Control

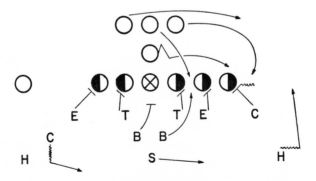

DIAGRAM 16-12
Even-Split-Control

Odd-Tackle-Gap Safety Blitz Assignments (See Diagrams 16-13 and 16-14.)

1. Safety: Slide into a safety blitz alignment to the split end side. With belly action to the split end, safety will slide laterally three steps and key the near back. If near back leads with belly action, safety will rotate up and support the quick corner to his inside. Belly action away, safety rotates back over deep middle zone.

2. Halfbacks: Halfback to split end side has same assignment as shown in previous diagrams. Halfback to tight end side will slide laterally three steps, keying the tight end and near back. From this position he will either cover the tight end man-to-man in the out zone or rotate up and support the corner from an inside position. If the tight end runs a post pattern the safety will cover him.

3. Corners: Both corners are aligned in their basic corner alignment off the line of scrimmage. They will key the near back. If he leads the option outside, the corner must rotate up and contain the play through a 4-Rotate technique. With action away the corner will check the back side streak zone for reverse action run or pass.

4. Ends: Both ends will align on the outside shoulder of either the tight end or the weak side tackle. End to tight end side will force the tight end to take an inside release, and he will contain the outside option. End to split end side will drive through the head of tackle and tackle the fullback. If tackle blocks out on him, he will slide outside to contain the quarterback, exchanging assignments with the linebacker.

5. Tackles: Middle tackle will use a control charge and key quarterback on belly action. He will slide to side of belly action and tackle the fullback from an inside position. Tackle to the strong side will drive through head of tackle and attempt to tackle the fullback from an outside position. If tackle blocks out on him, he will exchange assignments with the linebacker and contain the quarterback at the Tackle-Gap area.

6. Linebackers: Linebacker will key block of offensive tackle. If the tackle blocks down inside, linebacker will

move into the Tackle-Gap area and contain the quarter-back through our sliding technique. If tackle blocks out, linebacker will fill the Guard-Gap and tackle the fullback. Linebacker away from belly action will check the Center-Gap for counter action.

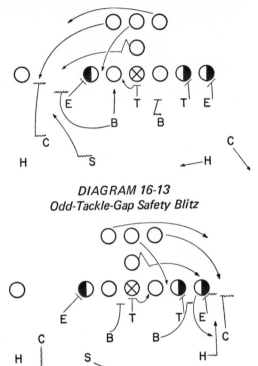

DIAGRAM 16-13
Odd-Tackle-Gap Safety Blitz

DIAGRAM 16-14
Odd-Tackle-Gap Safety Blitz

Odd-Safety-Tackle-Gap (See Diagram 16-15.)

The assignments for Odd-Safety-Tackle-Gap are identical to the Odd-Inside-Tackle-Gap as illustrated in Diagrams 16-9 and 16-10, the only difference being that the safety will contain the quarterback at the Tackle-Gap instead of the Power Corner. The halfback would have to cover the tight end man-to-man and the corner would rotate up to help the end contain the outside option. As previously indicated, this coverage would be used as a change-up to the wide side of the field.

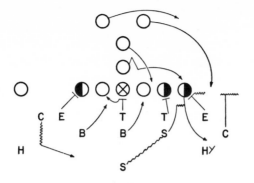

DIAGRAM 16-15
Odd-Safety-Tackle-Gap

COUNTER TRIPLE OPTION PLAYS

Houston University has developed an outstanding counter run and passing game off their Triple Option Series. We will illustrate one plan that could be used in defending against these moves.

Their basic counter play combination is a counter option play. We would key this play and cover it as follows.

The inside linebackers must key their near back and quarterback. Since this counter series develops very quickly, with the halfback and fullback taking only one counter jab-step each, the linebackers can afford to take one jab-step up with their inside leg. If the quarterback pivots away from the linebacker, he will

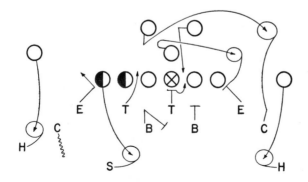

DIAGRAM 16-16
Odd-Tackle-Gap

immediately key his near-back for an inside counter. He will step up to meet the offensive guard with a Rip-up and then hold his ground. The back side linebacker will read the counter move of the trailing pitch man and then slide over to back up the counter action over the middle.

The back side end and corner immediately key for the counter option, with the end taking the quarterback and the corner taking the pitch man. We would use this same plan versus a counter option to the tight end side (Diagram 16-16).

Houston also runs a counter trap or crossbuck action versus an Odd alignment. The purpose of this play is to trap a hard-charging tackle. Again, as soon as our back side linebacker sees the quarterback pivot away from him with the fullback driving in the opposite direction, he will immediately step up and key the far back for crossbuck action. We coach the attacking tackle to check the fullback. If the fullback leaves, the tackle must hold his ground and prepare to meet the trapping guard. If this became a problem we would have the tackle use a Pinch technique instead. The onside linebacker keys through the guard to the near back, and if they both leave he will give a crossbuck call to alert back side linebacker and tackle.

Also note that the fullback slides over into a normal fullback position behind the quarterback. We would key this change in alignment for crossbuck action (Diagram 16-17).

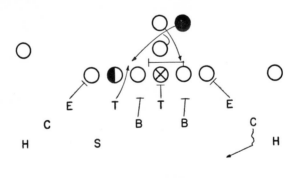

DIAGRAM 16-17
Odd-Tackle-Gap

Houston also runs effective counter passes that we would defend against as shown in Diagrams 16-18 and 16-19. It should be noted that with our man-to-man assignments versus Belly or counter action we can easily pick up the eligible pass receivers.

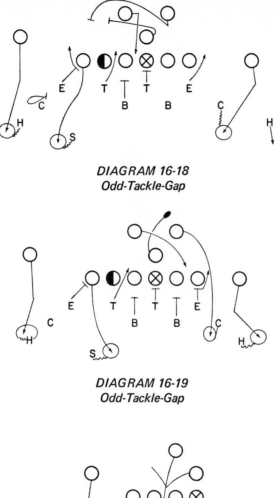

DIAGRAM 16-18
Odd-Tackle-Gap

DIAGRAM 16-19
Odd-Tackle-Gap

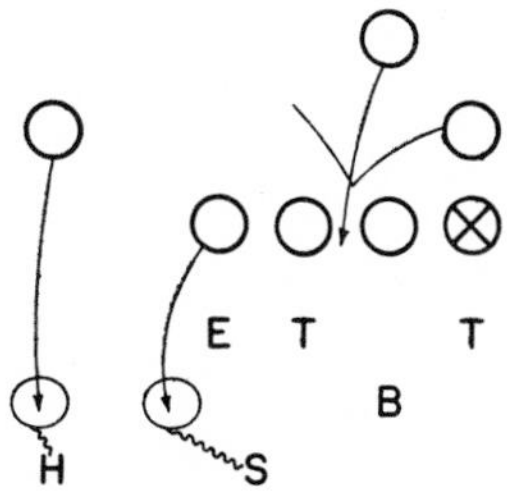

DIAGRAM 16-20
Quickie Pass

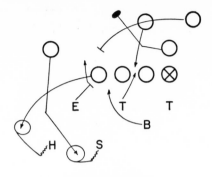

DIAGRAM 16-21
Dive Pass

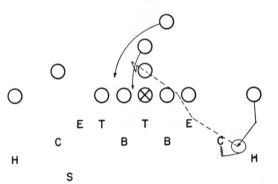

DIAGRAM 16-22
Throw Back Quickie

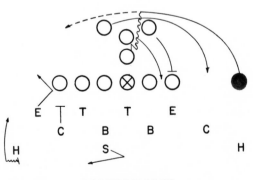

DIAGRAM 16-23
Flip Reverse

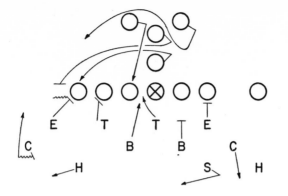

DIAGRAM 16-24
Odd-Tackle-Gap Safety Blitz

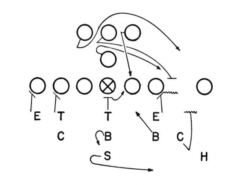

DIAGRAM 16-25
Odd-Inside-Tackle-Gap

Other forms of play action passes have been developed from the Triple Option Series to keep the defense off balance. We would defend against these passes as shown in Diagrams 16-20 through 16-22.

Another outside counter running play is the Flip Reverse. This play is a deep reverse to the split end. The halfback covering the split end keys him and yells "reverse" if the split end leaves to the back side. On reverse key the back side end, corner, and halfback rotate up in a 3-Rotate to cover the reverse (Diagram 16-23).

Wishbone-T Counter Option

We would use our basic back side coverage versus the Wishbone-T counter option. However, because of the fullback as a lead blocker outside, we would use our sliding outside containment technique. The back side linebacker would key the near halfback for the inside counter, and the back side end and corner would contain the outside counter option (Diagrams 16-24 and 16-25).

17

Defensing Favorite Play Combinations With the 53 Multiple

We have found over the years that most of our opponents run favorite play combinations from specific offensive formations. This is true because certain forms of offensive play action can be run better from specific formations. Examples would be as follows: sweep or roll-out plays run in a wing formation, quick toss and halfback trap plays run from a split-backs formation, and inside power plays run from a Power I formation. And, as previously indicated, specific blocking patterns are usually directly related to the offensive play action.

Another factor to consider is the fact that at the high school level the coach must mold his offense around the strengths of his existing personnel. He cannot recruit big fullbacks or speedy halfbacks from year to year as college coaches can. For example, if he has small but quick backs, he will probably design a quick hitting running game from the T formation.

Thus, in defensing favorite play combinations, we design defensive calls according to the anticipated formation, offensive play action, and the physical abilities of our opponent.

The following information will explain and illustrate how we defend against the most popular offensive running and pass play combinations.

SWEEP AND BOOTLEG

One of the most popular play combinations in football is the sweep and bootleg series. At the high school level this series is typically run from a split-end and wing formation. The sweep can generate much power towards the wing side, and the split end is a threat as a receiver to the back side to receive the bootleg pass.

The purpose of the sweep play is to form a wall of blockers in front of the ball carrier behind the line of scrimmage and then turn the corner en masse to overpower the defense. We believe that we must counter this strategy by breaking up the sweep before it is allowed to form and then turn the corner. This can be done by attacking our power corner inside to meet the lead blocker. It is his job to pressure the ball carrier behind the line of scrimmage to force the sweep play deep and to the outside. He is supported outside by a rotating halfback and to the inside by the power linebacker.

We have had success using two different defensive calls to the wing side. Versus the split-end wing formation, we meet strength with strength by moving our power corner up to the outside shoulder of the wingback to attack the sweep, and we drop the quick corner off to help double cover the split end. Versus teams that block one man to the inside we prefer an Even-End-Attack call. Versus teams that block straight ahead man-on-man, we prefer to use an Odd-Tackle-Gap call.

On sweep key the defenders must yell "sweep" and then execute their assignments as shown in Diagrams 17-1 and 17-2. Versus man-type blocking we usually break our power linebacker home free through the Tackle-Gap to either tackle the ball carrier for a loss or force him deep and outside.

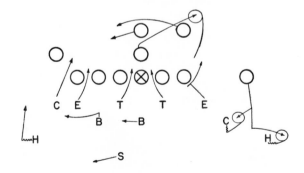

DIAGRAM 17-1
Even-End Attack

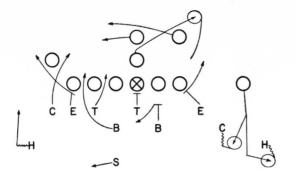

DIAGRAM 17-2
Odd-Tackle-Gap-Left-Control-Right

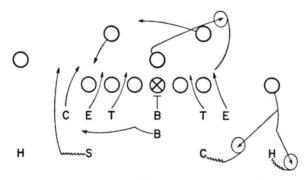

DIAGRAM 17-3
Odd-Double-End-Attack vs. Lombardi Sweep

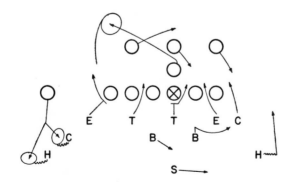

DIAGRAM 17-4
Odd-Tackle-Gap vs. Devaney's Sweep

The back side end will key and contain the quarterback on bootleg, and the back side corner and halfback will cover the split end for bootleg pass.

Two other exciting variations of the sweep bootleg combination play are the Lombardi sweep and Bob Devaney's (head coach of the University of Nebraska) short side sweep. Diagrams 17-3 and 17-4 show how we would defend against these fine play combinations.

TOSS AND TRAP

Another popular play combination is the Toss and Trap combination series from a split-backs Pro-offensive formation. From this formation, the offense can Quick Toss either way with a flanker and split end in position to crack-back on the contain man. The opposite halfback and guard, away from the toss action, can come back on an inside trap play from either direction. And, to complete this fine series, a fake toss play action pass can be effectively run to either the Flanker or Split-End sides.

The purpose of the Quick Toss play is to break a fast back to the outside as quickly as possible. This play features a pulling guard or tackle in front of the halfback, and if these men are allowed to turn the corner this play is difficult to stop. We believe that the best way to defend against the Quick Toss is to force the toss immediately and cut it off before it develops. This can be accomplished through an Odd-Double alignment. This call places two men, one at each of the flank areas, in position on the line of scrimmage to immediately cut off the toss play (Diagram 17-5).

If the split end or flanker moves into a crack-back blocking position, the contain men must move head-up on the split man to prevent the crack-back. The defensive halfback keys the crack-back position and moves up into a tight position to force the toss from an outside position. If the split receiver fakes crack-back and then runs a pass pattern, the inside safety or corner must cover him for pass (Diagram 17-6).

If the defense pursues too quickly to contain the toss play, the offense will counter inside with the inside halfback trap. And if the secondary rotates up too fast the quarterback will fake toss and throw a play action pass behind them.

To counter the trap play, we assign the middle linebacker to key through both guards to the halfbacks. The quarterback will

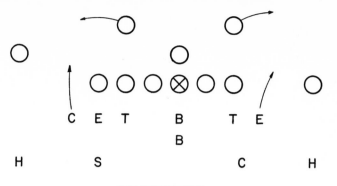

DIAGRAM 17-5
Odd-Double

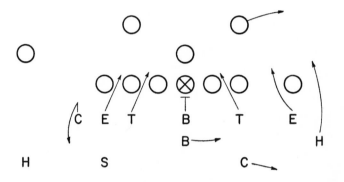

DIAGRAM 17-6
Quick Toss vs. Halfback Containment

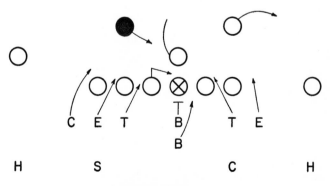

DIAGRAM 17-7
Odd-Double-Pinch vs. Trap

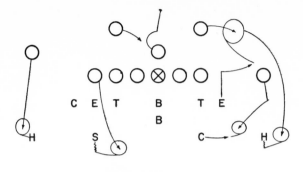

DIAGRAM 17-8
Toss Pass to Split End

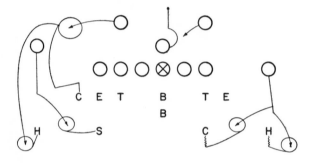

DIAGRAM 17-9
Toss Pass to Flanker

reverse pivot and hand off to the halfback, with the onside guard pulling to trap. On this key, the middle linebacker will fill tough just to the inside of the pulling guard's block. The tackles pinch down hard to the inside. If the guard to the tackle's side is pulling, he will attempt to get into his hip pocket to cut off the play from the inside. With both tackles pinching and an agile middle guard controlling the center it is very difficult to break the trap play up the middle (Diagram 17-7).

Toss play action passes would be covered as shown in Diagrams 17-8 and 17-9.

ROLL OUT SERIES

Pepper Rodgers, as the head coach at the University of Kansas (now head football coach at U.C.L.A.), ran one of the best designed Roll Out series in football. This series was run from a split-end wing formation. The advantage of this formation is that one man can be released from either side of the offensive line at the same time.

The purpose of this play is to isolate the defensive halfback and contain man to the side of Roll Out action. With one receiver running a deep route the halfback is forced to play pass. The contain man must make a choice to drop off and cover the second receiver out or move up and contain the quarterback run. The quarterback reads this option and either runs or throws. This series is complemented nicely with a fullback cut-back play just inside of the contain man, and the quarterback has the option of throwing back to two back side receivers. Thus on Roll action the quarterback can run, pass, or hand off.

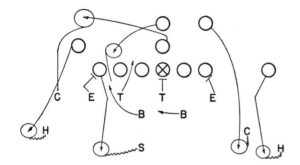

DIAGRAM 17-10
Odd-Tackle-Gap

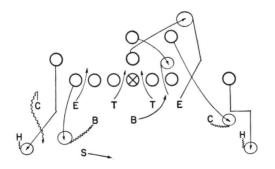

DIAGRAM 17-11
Even-Guard-Gap

We meet offensive strength with defensive strength by moving the power corner up to contain the quarterback and dropping off the quick corner to double cover the split end.

In defending against this outstanding series, we assign a man (man-to-man assignments) to cover each of the play options. Through this approach we never place a defensive man in a position to make a choice in coverage. For example, we will have a contain man assigned to the quarterback, two defensive backs to cover both receivers to Roll Out side, a linebacker is assigned to take the fullback cut-back play, and two secondary men are assigned to cover both back side receivers man-to-man. There is no guess work involved in our coverage and each man has one definite assignment to carry out.

We would use an Odd-Tackle-Gap and the Even-Guard-Gap calls. If the wide side of the field was to the wing side, we would use the Odd-Tackle-Gap call. With the wide side to the split end, we would use the Even-Guard-Gap call. On Roll Out key the defensive unit must yell "Roll Out" and then execute their assignment as illustrated in Diagrams 17-10 and 17-11.

I FORMATION PLAY COMBINATIONS

The I formation is probably the most popular offensive formation at the college and high school level. Many varied formations are run from the I formation backfield such as the slot, flanker, and Power I formations. However, at the high school level, we see more of the Power I formation.

The Power I formation can generate a tremendous power running attack up the middle. This is true because this formation places a fullback and an onside halfback in an ideal position to lead inside as blockers.

To meet strength with strength, we shift our defense into an Even-Tight call. From this alignment, we attack inside to meet offensive power with defensive power.

Basically, Power I teams like to drive off tackle to the tight end side with their onside halfback blocking the linebacker and the fullback trapping the defensive tackle. The tight end and tackle use a double-team block just inside the fullback's trap. To counter this blocking, we like to use an Even-Tight-Guard-Gap call. This call matches our Power Linebacker versus the smaller halfback. With the end attacking the Tackle-Gap, the tight end and tackle are forced to double team him. This leaves the Guard-Gap open for the Power Linebacker at attack. We want our Power Backer to meet the halfback across the line of scrimmage and break up the play at this point before it develops. As the offense adjusts their blocking we will mix in some Tackle-Gap calls with the end and power linebacker exchanging gaps (Diagram 17-12).

Power I teams like to run inside counters back to the split-end side with either the tailback off-guard or the halfback off-tackle. The Quick Backer keys the fullback. If the fullback leaves to the tight end side, he will automatically key counter at the Guard-Gap. The end keys the quarterback for bootleg and the back side corner and halfback cover the split end for pass (Diagram 17-13).

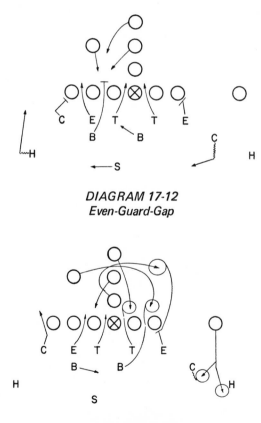

DIAGRAM 17-12
Even-Guard-Gap

DIAGRAM 17-13
Even-Tackle-Gap

Versus a Pro I formation that features the tailback in running to daylight, such as O.J. Simpson at U.S.C. of yesteryear, we would use our Looping technique.

The purpose of this offensive style of play is to get the ball back to the tailback, giving him plenty of room to pick his hole. The quarterback normally reverse pivots and takes the ball deep into the backfield to hand off to the tailback. The tailback darts to one side of the formation to pick an open hole. He usually has about three options to choose from. The fullback usually leads off-tackle and the linemen block man-on-man. If the defensive lineman penetrates or over-pursues, the offensive blocker can easily ride him in the direction of his charge to open up a hole for an exceptionally fast and agile tailback.

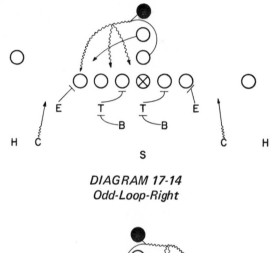

DIAGRAM 17-14
Odd-Loop-Right

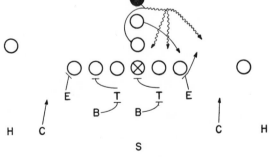

DIAGRAM 17-15
Even-Loop-Left

To counter this offensive play action, we would not penetrate or over-pursue. Rather, we would loop and hold our ground, covering every offensive blocker along the line of scrimmage. We also have excellent outside coverage with a 4-Rotate to both sides at the same time.

We would loop to the Split-End side from an Odd alignment and to the Flanker side from an Even alignment (Diagrams 17-14 and 17-15).

18

Covering Favorite Pass Plays
With the 53 Multiple

Modern offensive football coaches have been ingenious in their concoction of dynamic pass plays. Never before in the history of football have so many touchdown passes been thrown at the high school, college, and professional ranks. As a result, modern defensive football coaches have had to revise their secondary defenses to cope with this offensive threat. One of the newest innovations is the utilization of a 5-Deep secondary by professional football teams. However, they normally send in a fifth defensive back to replace a linebacker. Through our flexible defensive system, we can adjust to a 5-Deep secondary any time during a game without having to send in a substitute. This is a big advantage in adjusting to various forms of the passing game on the spot any time during a ball game. It only takes one mistake in defensive coverage to lose a game by one touchdown.

We believe that our five man secondary system provides some food for thought to be seriously considered by modern defensive coaches. Theoretically, when the 5-Man secondary is matched up with five eligible receivers the odds are evened up. So why not incorporate the 5-Man secondary system within the basic team defense? It can be easily accomplished by the utilization of a Quick Corner (actually a fourth defensive back) and a Power Corner that is utilized exactly like a single monster. The Power Corner has to have enough speed to cover a tight end or a fullback deep. And, in the opinion of the author, there are many men in football, at all levels, who have adequate size and speed to execute this assignment. It is logical to assume that if a Power Corner has to cover a tight end or fullback, why not put a tight end or fullback in this position.

Since we have incorporated this system within our team defense, we have led our league in pass defense four times in the past seven years. This feat was accomplished with average kids at the high school level. We believe that this is the proof of the pudding.

The advantages of the 5-Man secondary system are as follows:

1. The 5-Man secondary can easily adjust to the width of an offensive formation by dropping off either one or both corners into the seams between the defensive halfback and safety.
2. Inside linebackers never have to cover a fifth receiver deep, as this secondary always has a fifth secondary man in position to cover deep. This frees the linebacker to concentrate on the run and the short pass.
3. This 5-Man secondary has the capacity to cover the five eligible receivers man-to-man with hand-picked men who are trained to cover deep, releasing the linebackers from any pass coverage duties at all, which frees them to rush the passer.
4. This secondary places three men in position to cover three man Flood patterns to either side of the offensive formation, at the same time on a man-to-man basis.
5. The offense cannot force this 5-Man secondary into an unbalanced alignment to open up gaping holes to the back side secondary.
6. An offensive formation cannot force this secondary into single coverage on a split receiver as this secondary can easily adjust to double cover both split receivers at the same time.
7. We can cover the five deep zones, curl and flat zones, and still cover the swing and screen patterns underneath at the same time.

We realize that three and four deep secondaries can compensate and utilize their inside or outside linebackers to help their secondary in pass coverages. This is particularly true versus drop-back passes, which are easy to key and then react to. However, versus play action passes and reverse action passes linebackers have to be run-conscious first, which places them in a very difficult position. Our five man secondary is taught to key play action and reverse action passes first and run second. Another advantage is the fact that we hand pick men who have the ability and speed to cover deep, whereas many times an inside linebacker just does not have the speed to cover backs deep. An alert offense can take advantage of this situation, and through the deployment of a specific formation it can force the linebacker to man-to-man coverage on a back.

The following material will explain and illustrate how we cover various forms of modern pass plays.

COVERING FLOOD PASSES

The purpose of the Flood pass is to over-load a defensive zone to get a two-on-one advantage on a secondary back. Two man Flood patterns are successful against a defensive halfback aligned in a 3-Deep secondary. Three-man Flood patterns are successful against a defensive corner aligned in a 4-Deep secondary. Flood patterns are usually designed from split formations such as Slot, Wing, and Flanker formations with split-backs. From these formations receivers can be released in a hurry to flood a specific zone. With our defensive corners in position to either pick up a tight receiver or help inside on a split receiver, we can easily adjust to any form of a Flood pass. The following diagrams (18-1 to 18-4) will illustrate how the 5-Deep can cover various types of flood passes.

COVERING PASSES FROM SPREAD OR UNUSUAL FORMATIONS

Versus an unorthodox or spread formation, we automatically go into our Odd-Double call as shown in Diagrams 18-5, 18-6 and 18-7.

COVERING MAN-IN-MOTION PASSES

Many teams will use a man-in-motion to force a rotation in the secondary or to gain an extra one-man advantage to the strong

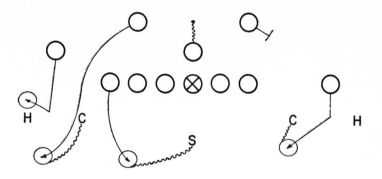

DIAGRAM 18-1
5-Deep vs. 3-Man Flood Pass

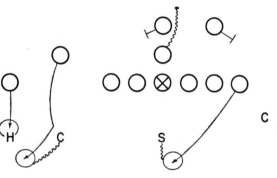

DIAGRAM 18-2
5-Deep vs. 2-Man Flood Pass

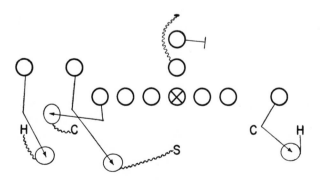

DIAGRAM 18-3
5-Deep vs. 3-Man Flood Pass

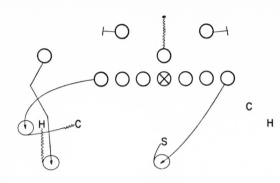

DIAGRAM 18-4
5-Deep vs. 2-Man Flood Pass

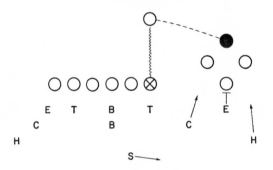

DIAGRAM 18-5
Double vs. Unorthodox Formation

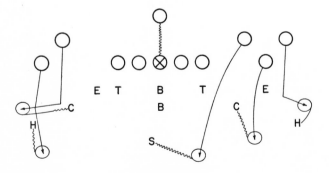

DIAGRAM 18-6
Double vs. Spread

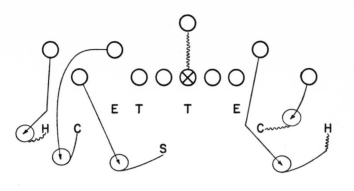

DIAGRAM 18-7
Odd vs. Shotgun Formation

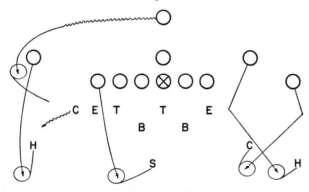

DIAGRAM 18-8
5-Deep vs. Man-in-Motion

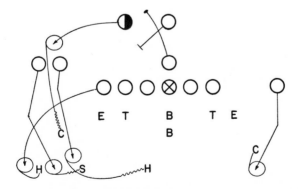

DIAGRAM 18-9
Odd-Double Pre-Rotate vs. Triple

side. We can easily counter both of these situations, because we always maintain balance in our back side defense with a corner dropped off, and the front side corner will drop off to cover the man-in-motion (Diagram 18-8).

With one man left in the backfield the defensive front automatically goes into a Control charge.

COVERING PASSES TO WIDE SIDE
OF FIELD

As previously indicated, we believe in favoring the wide side of the field. This is particularly true versus an opponent that over-loads the strength of their formation to the wide side. In Diagram 18-9 we illustrate a pass pattern thrown from a Triple Power formation to the wide side. In this situation, we would pre-rotate our secondary before the center snap. This would be done from an Odd-Double call. Through this approach, we can adjust our 5-Deep to the wide side of the field to get excellent coverage of pass or run.

COVERING UNDERNEATH SWING
AND SCREEN PASSES

We believe that one of the major weaknesses in modern day defenses is the coverage of the underneath passes in the Swing area. Split-backs Pro formation teams have had great success, through 5-Man patterns, hitting either the fullback or halfback on short swing or screen passes in the swing area. This is true because most of the standard defenses are forced to drop off their inside and outside linebackers to cover the hook and curl and flat zones, leaving the Swing areas vacated. To compensate for this weakness, we cover the curl zone to the split-end side with the quick corner and assign our quick backer to cover the halfback man-to-man for a swing, screen, or flat pass. We do not feel that the quick backer has to fly back to cover a hook zone to the split-end side, as there is not a tight end in position to run a hook pass. If the halfback runs a quick pass into this zone the quick backer can easily cover him through his man-to-man assignment. If the halfback runs a deep pattern either the quick corner or halfback will pick him up.

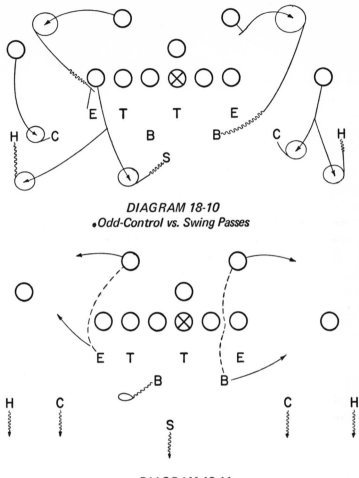

DIAGRAM 18-10
•Odd-Control vs. Swing Passes

DIAGRAM 18-11
Save-the-Game Pass Defense

To the flanker side, the defensive end is assigned to key and then cover the fullback for a swing or screen pass. The power linebacker has the hook zone, and the power corner covers the curl zone to the flanker side. (Refer to Diagram 18-10 for our Swing coverage.)

SAVE-THE-GAME PASS DEFENSE

We would go into this defensive call late in the game when it is obvious that our opponent must throw the long bomb to defeat us. We align in 5-Deep with the corners and halfbacks ten yards deep. The safety is fifteen yards deep. They play zone pass defense, not letting a receiver behind them in their zone. Versus Roll-Out or Play Action passes, they play a 4-Rotate. The linebackers and ends would play their regular pass defensive coverages. They would be particularly alert for screen or draw.

The safety is the key to this defense. He must stay deeper than the ball or the deepest receiver at all times. He is the last resort man, and it is mandatory that he is in position to play the field, in width and depth, so that he can make that desperation tackle of a break-away receiver (Diagram 18-11).

19

Goal Line Defensive Coverage
From the 53 Multiple

GOAL LINE COVERAGES VERSUS RUN

Versus the run in Goal Line situations (with our opponent inside our ten yard line), we go into an Even-Tight-Goal-Line call. This alignment is a 65 alignment which fits in quite well with our basic defensive assignments and coverages.

The defensive tackles and ends align in their tight alignment. It is their assignment to penetrate the inside gaps to seal off the Center and Guard gaps. They will execute their goal line technique as previously described.

The safety moves up into an attacking or middle linebacker position. His depth is dependent upon field position. On the one yard line he would be up tight in a normal linebacker position. From this position, he plays like a middle linebacker keying the flow of the ball and then filling inside. We key him on a specific back when we have good tendencies on an opponent. On an obvious outside play he will take an angle back and prepare to support the halfback from an inside position.

The inside linebackers move into a linebacker position on the inside shoulder of the tight end with their outside foot back. From this alignment they will step up with their outside foot and shed through the head of the tight end, using a Rip-up technique, and then step inside with their inside foot to cover the inside Tackle-Gap. If the tight end tries to block down on him, the linebacker must hold his ground and fight through his head to the outside. If flow is away, the inside linebacker will hold and check for counter as he gradually rotates back over the short center zone.

Corner men are aligned in a tight alignment on the outside shoulder of the tight end. From this alignment they will use their basic shedding and containment technique through the head of the tight end. If flow is coming to him, he will play his regular outside technique. If flow is away from him, he will play his regular back side technique, keying for bootleg or reverse and then rotating back to out zone.

Halfbacks align in an outside corner alignment. The depth of the halfbacks will depend upon field position. On the goal line they must play head-up and tight on top of the split receiver. Mid-field they would play off the split receiver from five to six yards. If flow is towards the halfback, he will key the tight end for two counts, and if he is still blocking, he will move up fast to help contain the outside. If flow is away, he must key the tight end man-to-man and then gradually rotate over the Center zone on a release call from the corner.

The secondary will apply our basic rules of coverage in adjusting to split formations. Versus a wing formation, the corner must adjust to the outside shoulder of the wingback and the linebacker must play head-up on the tight end. We shift the safety man over behind the defensive end to support the linebacker at the Tackle-Gap read (Diagram 19-1).

Versus a split-end formation, we move the linebacker up to contain and drop off the corner to double cover the split end, or we can keep the corner up to contain and move the linebacker into his normal linebacking position (Diagrams 19-2 and 19-3).

Versus a Flanker formation, we shift the safety into a Safety Blitz position as shown in Diagram 19-4. Versus a Slot or Triple formation, the corner will drop off into his normal adjustment and we cover the inside running game as previously indicated (Diagrams 19-5 and 19-6).

GOAL LINE COVERAGES VERSUS
PASS

Versus a tight offensive formation the secondary, on drop back key, will fly back to their basic pass defense zones (Diagram 19-7).

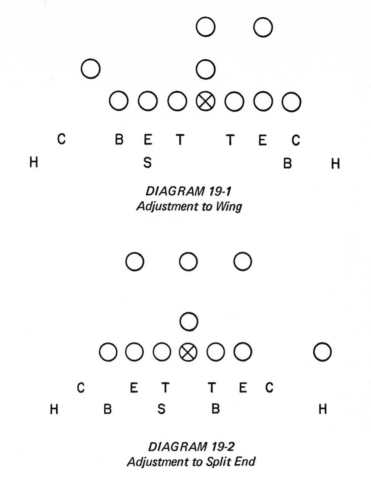

DIAGRAM 19-1
Adjustment to Wing

DIAGRAM 19-2
Adjustment to Split End

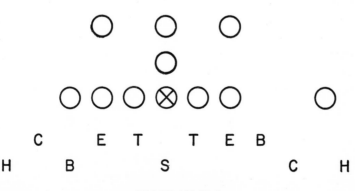

DIAGRAM 19-3
Adjustment to Split End

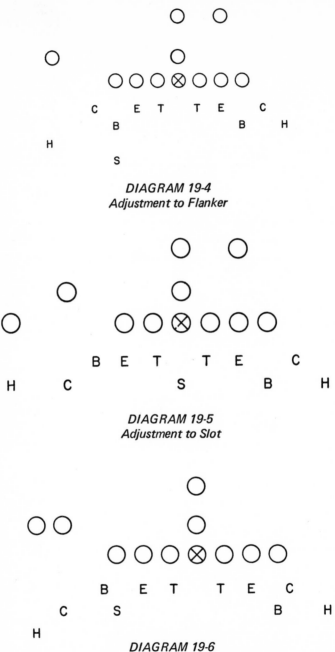

DIAGRAM 19-4
Adjustment to Flanker

DIAGRAM 19-5
Adjustment to Slot

DIAGRAM 19-6
Adjustment to Triple

The inside linebackers will step up and Rip-up the tight ends, forcing them to the outside while covering on a man-to-man basis to the inside hook zone.

The corners will step up, making contact on the outside shoulder of the tight ends and then move as quickly as possible to the Flat zones.

The three deep backs will cover their deep zones, and the ends on pass key must change their charge to the outside so that they are in position to rush and contain the quarterback.

Versus split formations, the secondary will observe our rules of adjustment, and they will adjust in the same manner as described for Goal Line adjustments for the run. From our adjustments to split formations, we automatically drop off and play zone pass defense on drop back key. However, on or near the goal line defensive halfbacks will have to play split receivers very tight as there is very little depth in field area. Also, they must get an inside position on the receiver. The Look-in pass is a very effective pattern on the goal line area as the quarterback has a good angle to hit the receiver and it is a quick pass. The halfback must not let the split receiver get through him to the inside, forcing him to the outside. The out pattern is difficult to throw near the goal line as the outside angle between the passer and the receiver is very shallow. If the halfback maintains his inside position and plays the ball properly, he should be able to easily slap the ball down. He must be careful about intercepting the ball in this area, because if he is tackled near the goal line he will place his team in poor field position. Refer to Diagrams 19-7 through 19-12 for pass coverages versus split formations.

Versus Roll Out, we use an Eagle containment on the quarterback. On key, the linebacker will step up and Rip-up the tight end and then release to the outside to contain the quarterback. The corner will fly to the flat zone with the rest of the secondary playing their deep zones. We also use the 4-Rotate versus play action passes, the only difference being that on pass key the linebacker will move back to his hook zone as he will not have to contain the quarterback on play action passes.

In the middle of the field we prefer to use the Even-Tight-Tackle-Gap call. The safety is free to play his deep Center zone in case of a play action pass deep. The inside linebacker will generally

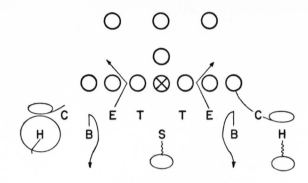

DIAGRAM 19-7
Zone vs. Tight Formation

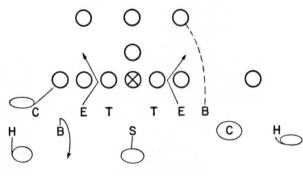

DIAGRAM 19-8
Zone vs. Split End

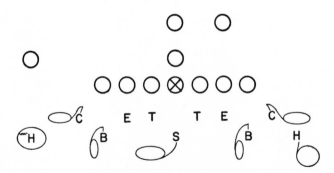

DIAGRAM 19-9
Zone vs. Flanker

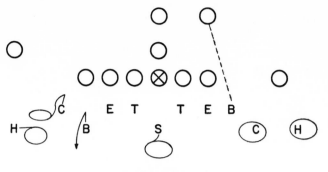

DIAGRAM 19-10
Zone vs. Pro

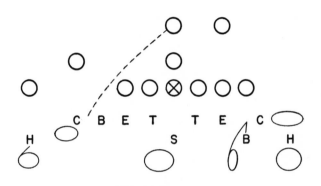

DIAGRAM 19-11
Zone vs. Slot

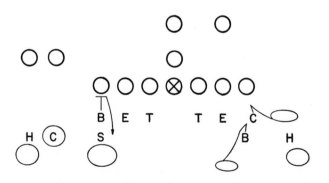

DIAGRAM 19-12
Zone vs. Triple

key on a specific back in short yardage, but his area of responsibility is the Tackle-Gap.

We sell our men on the idea that our opponent must not score on us inside our 10 yard line. At the close of our Tuesday's scrimmage, in reviewing our defensive game plan, we put the ball on the 10 yard line and give the demonstration team four downs to score. We use the over-load principle by giving the offensive team two extra blockers. The offensive team or third unit then tries to score with 13 men. When our defensive unit holds them without a score, which is usually the case, we praise our defensive unit for a job well done. We believe that this motivational technique helps to build team confidence. The coach should use a quick whistle in this drill, and he must be careful not to prolong this drill; otherwise the opportunity for injuries can be great.

20

Selecting and Training the
53 Multiple Defensive Quarterback

SELECTING THE QUARTERBACK

The defensive quarterback must possess leadership qualities in the same fashion as an offensive quarterback. He must display confidence in himself and his teammates so that he will make defensive calls with authority and self-assurance. A good defensive quarterback has the ability to ignite fire and enthusiasm within a defensive unit, and it is this type of team attitude that is necessary to make that last ditch stand to stop an opponent on the goal line.

A fine defensive quarterback will have the complete respect of his teammates. This respect is vital, in our opinion, to the success of a defensive unit. We believe that good leadership breeds good unit morale and pride, which will certainly enhance our chances of achieving success as a defensive unit. In order to be a fine team leader, the defensive quarterback must possess intelligence, athletic ability, and a burning desire to succeed.

Intelligence is an important consideration. This is particularly true if the defensive system is a multiple system such as our defensive system. He must have the intelligence to select the best possible call to meet the specific game situation. It does not require a genius to be the defensive signal caller. A player with average intelligence and good football sense can make an excellent signal caller. Some football players have a natural football sense that seems to give them the innate ability to diagnose game situations and then be at the right place at the right time. This type of football sense is an ideal characteristic for the quarterback to have.

Physical ability is also an important factor that must be considered by the defensive coach. Players generally respect a man who has outstanding playing ability. Such a man is capable of making the big defensive play in a key situation. This type of indirect leadership can be inspirational to his teammates.

Desire and fire are other qualities that we look for in our quarterback. We prefer a man who hustles 110% throughout a football game, and has the ability to talk it up and pat his teammates on the butt when the going gets tough. Such a man will indeed inspire his teammates to greater heights.

Generally, we select the Power Linebacker to make our defensive calls. To play this position our man must have size, strength, and good athletic ability. His very presence indicates that he is a man to be reckoned with. From his middle position he is in an ideal alignment to recognize offensive formations, so he can check and adjust defensive calls. Both sides of the defensive line can hear his calls from this central vantage point.

The defensive safety is also ideally located in the center of the defensive secondary to make secondary calls, and he will remain in the secondary to make adjustments when necessary. Our safety man must be one of our better all-around men so that he is also well suited to this assignment.

TRAINING THE QUARTERBACK

The defensive coach must meet with the quarterback regularly in the same manner that the offensive coach meets with the offensive quarterback. This is true because the quarterback must understand the basic theories behind our multiple defense, and he should know the basic assignments of every man on the Forcing Unit. He must also know when to make each defensive call and the purpose of each call. As he meets regularly with the defensive coach, he must make appropriate notes in his defensive notebook.

During the first quarterback meeting of the season, before the coach gets into the specifics of the Multiple 53 Defense, he must first familiarize the quarterback with the basic theories behind our defensive system of play. At this time the defensive coach will cover the advantages and objectives of our defense as listed in Chapter I. Also, the defensive coach must be sure that the quarterback understands our jumping defensive strategy, as this concept is the basis behind our multiple defensive system or defensive calls. This is true because the defense will jump from one alignment to another alignment, from down to down, in adjusting to an opponent according to game situations. In selling our defense to the quarterback, we stress the fact that we will do a thorough job of scouting each opponent and that we will provide the best possible call to meet each specific game situation.

Furthermore, we stress the point that our multiple defense is one basic defense with variations in calls, rather than several different basic defenses. This helps to simplify the system so the quarterback can easily cement the basic calls together into one neat package.

During the early season, before the first football game, all of the basic defensive calls must be covered in practice. Each time a specific call is given to the team, the defensive quarterback should meet individually with the defensive coach for a special session relating to the purpose of the call. The "Field General" must talk like a coach on the field, and this additional attention to details is necessary to give him the extras that could make the difference between winning or losing.

In preparation for those initial meetings with the quarterback, it is very important that we simplify our multiple system so that it is easy for the quarterback to understand. Thus, we minimize what we are doing and at the same time maintain the flexibility we need to adjust to game situations. First, we limit the number of calls. The basic calls that we teach the quarterback are the Even, Even-Tight (Pro and Goal Line variations), Odd (Inside variation), and Odd-Double with the Inside' variation. Although there are other possibilities in defensive alignments, as previously indicated, we have found that these specific alignments fullfill our defensive requirements and represent our basic multiple defense.

We also boil down the call system because we have found that by eliminating unnecessary words it is much easier for the quarterback to make calls. For example, we align in an Even alignment as a starting point, then jump into the other basic alignments. When we want to jump into an Even-Tight call all the quarterback needs to call is Tight. If we want a Pro or Goal Line variation, he would call Tight-Pro or Tight-Goal Line. It is not necessary to repeat Even again since we start with an Even first, and the Tight defensive variations are only associated with an Even alignment. The quarterback calls Double instead of Odd-Double since we only use the Double variation as an Odd alignment. A variation that we use with the Odd or Double calls is an Odd-Inside or a Double-Inside.

To summarize, the following basic calls make up our Multiple 53 Defense and the quarterback must be taught these calls as follows: Even, Tight, Tight-Pro, Tight-Goal Line, Odd, Odd-Inside, Double, and Double-Inside.

The following material will illustrate how we teach our basic calls to the quarterback in sequential order. We follow this same progression in teaching the basic calls to our defensive unit.

We begin by teaching the defensive quarterback how the Forcing Unit aligns in an Even alignment. We start with the Even as a middle of the road alignment, as it is easier for the Forcing Unit to jump inside to a Tight alignment or outside to a Double alignment from this middle position. As the quarterback learns the basic calls he also learns the jumping system at the same time, as shown in Diagrams 20-1 to 20-4.

To simplify the teaching process, we begin by showing the quarterback how the Forcing Unit aligns first. As we explain the reasons for these changes in alignment as related to specific calls,

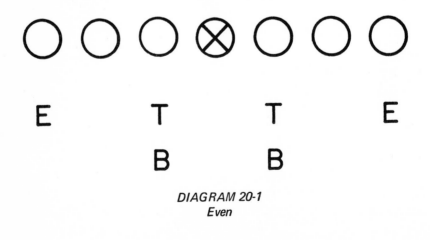

DIAGRAM 20-1
Even

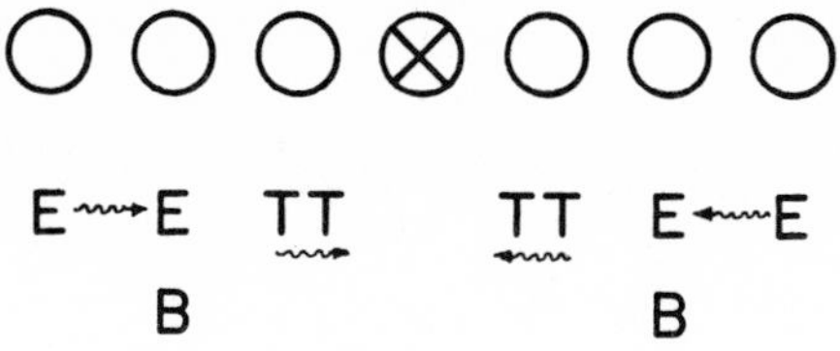

O O O ⊗ O O O

E ⤳E TT   TT E⬳E

B   B

DIAGRAM 20-2
Tight

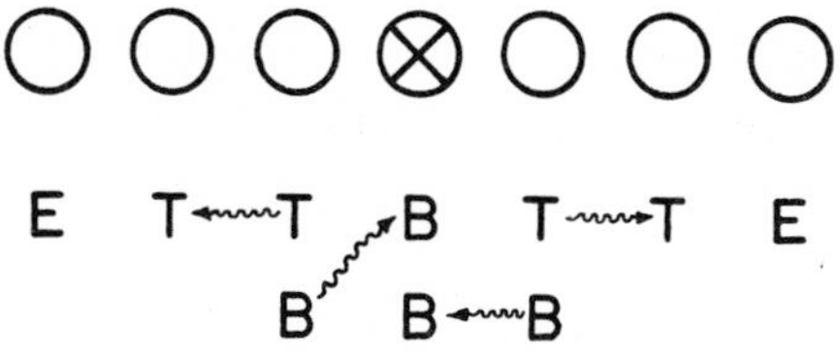

O O O ⊗ O O O

E   T⬳T ↗B T⤳T   E

B   B⬳B

DIAGRAM 20-3
Double

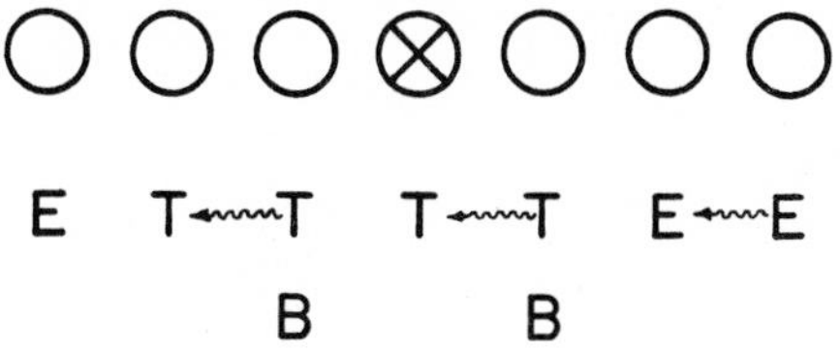

O O O ⊗ O O O

E   T⬳T   T⤳T   E⬳E

B   B

DIAGRAM 20-4
Odd

we also include the alignment of the Containing Unit. The alignment of the Containing Unit complements the Forcing Unit, which brings to light the specific purpose of each call. Next we illustrate to the quarterback when we will use each of the basic calls according to game situations such as offensive formations, anticipated offensive play action, field position, and down and yardage.

We begin by illustrating our basic calls versus tight offensive formations. We meet the Tight-T, Power-I, and the Wing-T. Although all of our opponents use a split end variation from these alignments, we still begin by defensing two tight ends. Basically, we teach our defensive quarterback to make defensive calls according to either running or passing down situations. Play action passes are considered within the running down category. We have a basic rule of thumb that we use as a guide in calling defenses according to down and yardage. This rule states that 1-10, 2-8 or under, 3-6 or under, and 4-3 or under are considered running downs, and 1-15, 2-9 or more, 3-7 or more and 4-4 or more are considered passing downs. This basic rule is altered if our opponent's tendencies indicate a difference from our basic down and yardage rule. However, in most cases we have found that a typical high school team will fall into the above categories.

Our first defensive priority is that we must meet offensive strength with proportionate defensive strength. And second, we must prepare to meet the anticipated offensive play action. We begin by teaching our basic calls for running down situations versus tight formations.

Versus a Tight-T formation that features deceptive inside faking and play options such as the Belly Series, we would use a Double-Inside call. We show the quarterback how we would move the corners inside to meet offensive strength with defensive strength in a man-to-man basis with three inside linebackers in position to meet three inside running backs (Diagram 20-5).

Versus the Power-I formation that features a power running attack up the middle we would use a Tight call. This call would illustrate how we can meet the strength of this formation to the inside by moving the Forcing Unit inside to meet strength with strength (Diagram 20-6).

If the sweep, toss, or roll out plays are featured from these tight formations, we would jump into an Even call. This call places the corners in position to contain these outside plays (Diagram 20-7).

Next we would explain that in running down situations versus tight formations the Forcing Unit would use the attack and pinch techniques. The secondary would use 3-Rotate or Eagle containment techniques. At this time we would review our system for calling the Attack calls, and then apply these calls to the above game situations. Examples would be as follows: Double-Tackle-Gap, Tight-Guard-Gap, and Even-End-Attack (Diagrams 20-5 to 20-7).

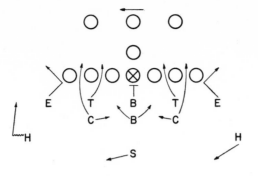

DIAGRAM 20-5
Double Tackle Gap

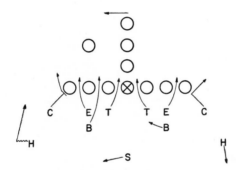

DIAGRAM 20-6
Tight-Guard Gap

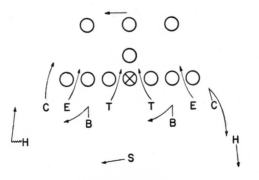

DIAGRAM 20-7
Even-End Attack

As a change-up to confuse offensive blocking, we always include alternate calls within every game plan. We would illustrate the Double-Pinch and Even-Pinch in conjunction with the above calls.

On a running down situation, we would use an Even-Slant to the wide side of the field with a 4-Rotate in the secondary, and to the short side we would use a Pinch technique with a 3-Rotate in the secondary. This call would illustrate to the quarterback how we can take advantage of field position.

If our opponent is deep in his own territory, we would illustrate to our quarterback how he would use either a Double or a Tight attacking call with the thought of forcing a fumble. The over-load principle and stressing the fact that we should be able to break a linebacker through a gap "home free" would be also be stressed at the point.

On a short yardage situation in the middle of the field, we would call a Tight-Tackle-Gap call, and inside our 10 yard line we would call a Tight-Goal Line call.

We would also remind the quarterback that we must key for play-action passes on every running down. The play of the halfback and corner in taking their three steps to key through the tight receivers to the quarterback would be stressed as an important coaching point.

Before moving on to long yardage situations, we would review our back side coverages versus inside counters, bootleg, and throw back passes from tight formations.

Versus a tight formation, we would use an Even-Control-Pass-Defense on a passing down and key for screen and draw.

Next, we would show the quarterback how we adjust our corner to the outside shoulder of the wingback to meet strength with strength, and we would illustrate our basic attacking calls versus this alignment, such as the Even-End-Attack, Double-End-Attack, or the Odd-Tackle-Gap calls.

After covering the defensive calls versus tight formations, we begin teaching our defensive quarterback how we will adjust versus split formations. First, we explain how the contain man must adjust to a split man in the crack-back blocking position to prevent this block. Then we open up the offensive formation to split end, flanker, slot, triple, spread, and unusual formations.

To meet strength with strength, we illustrate how we drop off our corner versus split-end, flanker, and slot formations. We stress the reasons why this corner adjustment is so important at the corner area versus the Belly Option, Roll Out, 3-Man Flood passes, and in double covering an outstanding split receiver. The use of the 4-Rotate and Eagle coverages are explained in conjunction with the Slant, Control, and Attacking techniques that are used with these secondary coverages. Again, the back side coverages and play action pass coverages versus split formations would be illustrated and explained to the quarterback.

Versus a Pro formation team that runs effective Sweep or Toss plays, we illustrate the Safety Blitz containing technique from the Double-End-Attack call.

The reasons for the Odd-Control-Pass-Defense and the Even attacking defenses versus split formations on a passing down would be explained in detail. Other basic calls such as slanting to the wide side, tight calls in short yardage and goal line situations, and attacking an opponent deep in his own territory are always basic calls that are used versus split formations as well as tight formations.

As the offensive formation splits out into Triple, Spread, or Unusual formations, we show the quarterback how to call and utilize the Double adjustment as described in this text.

And, last but not least, we would diagram and explain our Save-the-Game pass defense to the quarterback.

GAME PREPARATIONS

After the season begins, the defensive quarterback should meet with his defensive coach on a Monday morning to get the defensive game plan to be practiced in preparation for the next opponent. We practice our defensive game plan versus a demonstration unit on Tuesday of each week, so on Tuesday morning before school begins the defensive coach meets with the defensive quarterback to review his defensive calls.

The coach who has scouted the opponent should be in charge of preparing the demonstration team. On Mondays we provide this coach and his demonstration team time to run through the opponent's offense.

During this defensive practice, we set up all of the possible game situations that we anticipate from our opponent according to our scouting report. It is the defensive quarterback's responsibility, on his own, to make the right call for each game situation. If he makes a mistake the defensive coach must correct him immediately after the play is run and then run the same situation with the quarterback giving the proper call.

We scrimmage during this practice session. We use a quick whistle, however, and we are careful not to extend this scrimmage any longer than necessary. This control is necessary to prevent injuries.

During the last practice, the day before our game, we walk through our defensive game plan. During this session the defensive quarterback is quizzed according to game situations. Defensive quarterbacks enjoy this practice as they personally call each defensive call with much confidence and enthusiasm. We want our defensive quarterback to feel that we have a big advantage over our opponent because we know what he is going to do. Through this approach our man gains much confidence and satisfaction as he directs our defensive unit with the anticipation of destroying the enemy. As a result of this approach, we have been able to develop outstanding spirit and team morale on the part of our defensive unit.

As previously indicated, we would align in an Even alignment first on each down. If the call in the huddle is not an Even call, we would jump into the call given in the huddle as soon as the quarterback gets under the center. Example could be an Odd-Tackle-Gap call. In this situation the defense would come out in an Even alignment and then jump into an Odd alignment. If we can create confusion, we will do a lot of jumping. If the offense gets off on "Set" or on a quick count, we might not be able to jump. In this case we will immediately come out into the call given in the huddle.

Normally we will have five or six calls planned for each game. We always have our standard calls to meet the basic game situations, as previously noted, and we have at least two basic calls that are designed to meet the "bread-and-butter" plays of our opponent. We have found that we need at least one change-up call to keep the offense honest when they adjust to our number one defensive call. And, of course, because of the flexibility of our multiple defense we can easily design new calls, if necessary, to meet game situations we did not anticipate.

Also, if the offensive quarterback uses an audible system, we will try to confuse his audible calls by moving our corners in and out. For example, if the offensive quarterback audibles a quick pass to the split receiver when he sees our corner in an attacking alignment, we will try to sucker the quarterback into this audible and then jump the corner back into his basic corner position to stop this pass.

THE FIELD GENERAL IN ACTION

During a game the defensive quarterback is responsible for making each call. First, he must align the defensive huddle. We have our defensive quarterback stand mid-way in front of the defensive unit. The Forcing Unit stands in front facing the quarterback, with the Containing Unit in the second row facing the quarterback (Diagram 20-8). Quarterback is facing the line of scrimmage.

C   H   S   H   C
B   E   T   T   E

PB

DIAGRAM 20-8
Defensive Huddle

The Power Backer will make a first call and then repeat it to be sure each man understands the call. The safety man can call out the secondary coverage or remind the containing unit about the coverage to be used. However, in most cases the secondary coverage is automatically dependent upon the Forcing Unit's call. An example of a call would be Even-Slant-Right — Even-Slant-Right, Ready — Desire. On the command "Desire" each man claps his hands together in unison and breaks the huddle.

We feel the key to a hustling and hard hitting unit is Desire, and we explain the meaning of Desire in the following terms.

Desire means that each man must have a burning need to be the best possible football player he can possibly be on each defensive play. To accomplish this goal he must hustle 110% on each play, never loafing or quitting until the play is over, have the courage to stick his head into a ball carrier to make a vicious tackle, have the spirit and enthusiasm to become tougher when the going gets tougher, and have the heart and mental toughness to endure and conquer physical pain and then come back tougher on the next play.

We believe that we sell our defensive unit on the meaning of Desire, and as a result we usually have great team morale and pride within our defensive unit.

EXAMPLE OF GAME PLAN

We would like to include a brief sketch of a game plan to show the reader-coach what our typical game plan looks like.

A summary of our scouting report indicates that our opponent runs from a split-end wing formation. His bread-and-butter plays are a sweep and roll out to the wing side and an inside belly series to the split-end side.

To meet strength with strength we would use an Even-End-Attack call as our basic call, with the Power Corner up to attack the wing side and the Quick Corner dropped off to double cover the split end. Maintaining this same defensive strength, we would use a Tight-Tackle-Gap call as an alternate call (Diagrams 20-9 and 20-10).

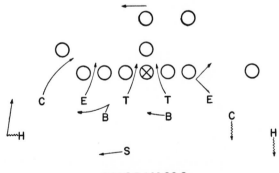

DIAGRAM 20-9
Even-End-Attack

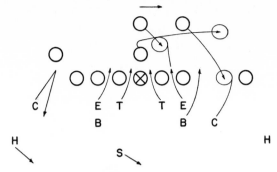

DIAGRAM 20-10
Tight-Tackle-Gap

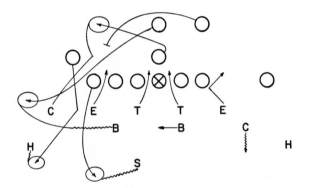

DIAGRAM 20-11
Eagle Coverage vs. Roll out

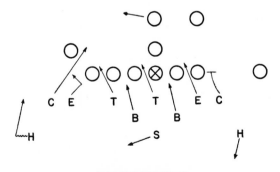

DIAGRAM 20-12
Slant-to-Wide Side

We would attack the sweep with our basic attack plan with a 3-Rotate in the secondary. Our opponent runs a 3-Man flood pattern on their roll out to the wing. Thus, on roll-out key, we would use an Eagle Flat coverage with a 4-Rotate in the secondary, as shown in Diagram 20-11.

To the split end side, the Quick Backer would key the fullback and take him on the inside belly action. The end would be assigned to the quarterback keeper outside, and the Quick Corner is assigned to cover the near halfback on their belly pass in the flat. On the Tight-Tackle-Gap call the end will take the fullback and the quick backer will take the quarterback on the outside keeper.

Other basic calls would be as follows:

1. Odd-Control-Pass Defense to be used on passing downs.
2. Tight-Goal Line to be used inside the 10 yard line.
3. Odd-Slant to be used to the wide side of the field with the corner attacking if the wing is to the wide side (Diagram 20-12).

Other standard calls that automatically become a part of our game plan are the Double call versus a Spread or unusual formation, the Even call versus a tight formation during a passing down, and the Save-the-Game pass defensive call as described in this text. We always have these calls in the wings in case we need them for adjustment.

Index